Xelie's Gift

A story of transformation and inspiration from this life to the next.

By

Michele McGuire

Photographs by the author, except where indicated.

Michele McGuire

The photographs used in the book have various copyright dates that are held by the individual photographer or licensing library and are used with permission.

For information on obtaining fine art prints of Bob Degus' images, contact him at his website, www.BobDegus.com

Book and text Copyright © 2014 Michele McGuire

Second Printing

ISBN-13: 978-1503339101

ISBN-10: 1503339106

Acknowledgements

A special thanks to Bob Degus for
bringing "Xelie's Gift" to life. Without his beautiful artistic
design, stunning photos and technical expertise the book would have
lived simply as pages of text. My eternal gratitude for his help, and
for his continued friendship and support. I count myself among the
lucky to have a friend like him.

Michele McGuire

Table of Contents

Introduction

I have loved animals ever since I can remember. Growing up, I spent endless hours begging my parents to allow me a variety of companions ranging from dogs and cats to gerbils, guinea pigs, ferrets, raccoons, horses and fish. My pleas to add countless critters to our household sometimes fell on deaf ears, and rightfully so. As I look back at my youth, had I been given free reign, I would have had my family living in a zoo.

When I entered my adult years and began to pursue a career, apartment living, long hours spent at work and the constraints of city life seemed incompatible with responsible animal cohabitation. What kind of life would it be for a dog or cat to spend countless hours confined and alone?

In the ten years that followed, I never fully adapted to living without the company of an animal friend. There was a hole in my life, an empty spot that I vowed to someday fill once again.

The dream finally materialized in 1993 when my future husband and I moved in to a small house with a sizeable city yard. It wasn't long before we had two additional family members living in our household – Sprocket and Dot, gentle, loving Newfoundlands.

From that point forward to the present, animals have been an integral part of my life. Dogs became the dominant species in my world. They were dear friends, companions, playmates and later working partners.

And as anyone knows who has ever had a variety of dogs in their life, or multiple dogs at one time, or dogs with whom they enjoy activities such as agility, herding or flyball -- as all of you know, now and then one character emerges who is exemplary, and special above and beyond the norm.

In my life, I have been blessed with a number of exceptional canine friends and working partners; animals whom I've loved dearly and held in high regard. But amongst all these wonderful companions, the most remarkable of all was a Picardy Shepherd named Xelie.

The inspiration for this book and countless hours of deep introspection, Xelie was a spirit beyond compare, one of brilliance, humor, wisdom, artistry and love. Under me, she had always been the leader, the alpha of my pack, but never in my wildest dreams did I expect her to reverse the roles and become my leader, my teacher.

"Xelie's Gift" is our story; a story of transformation and inspiration, a story of everlasting love and friendship that continues, even now, beyond death, into the future, forever.

Dedicated to

Xelie

April 13, 2001 to July 5, 2014

Xelie, pronounced, Zelly *photo by Bob Degus*

1.

The making of an ALPHA

I didn't know Xelie was sick.

She was a magnificent creature with dark eyes that danced a fine line between playfully warm and seriously in charge. Even at thirteen years old, she was hands down the alpha of my pack when I was not around, and sometimes even when I was...

She'd remind me to pay attention so balance would be maintained and so no one would get hurt. She was the best leader I have ever known, canine, human, or otherwise, and I have known quite a few. Consummately

Lucy, in a moment of calm.   *photo by Bob Degus*

fair and generous, she had nothing to prove. Her power rose from an inner wisdom about what was just, loving and good for all. She had learned from her puppyhood under an erratic, sometimes violent predecessor named Lucy. A ruler who had spent her first five puppy months, homeless, fighting for her life on the streets of L.A. She'd had to be tough to survive, and the imprint of the experience never left her.

A rescue, Lucy had quickly risen to power through ferocity and displays of frightening power. She was a dictator, laying claim to every toy, every dog bed, every aspect of her new kingdom. And God help any of her subjects who failed to comply, either purposely or inadvertently.

Having no prior experience with a creature such as this, we quickly came to realize we needed professional help. Sadly, for Xelie, she was a victim of our learning curve.

Xelie and Lucy seemed to get along so nicely at first. But we all quickly learned that Lucy, the leader that Xelie so wanted to revere, would be an exciting playmate at one moment, then an instant later try to rip her to shreds. After the trauma of two such experiences, at less than six

2

months old, Xelie and Lucy were kept separate forever.

And from this point forward, Xelie decided a leader should be generous, they should look after and care for their pack, never dominate through fear and violence simply to indulge their own greed and feed their lack of self-esteem.

Newfoundlands, Sprocket and Dot   *photo by Terry McGuire*

Before Xelie reached the end of her first year, the two other aged members of her group, peace loving Newfoundlands, Sprocket and Dot, passed away, leaving Xelie, at the tender age of eight months old, alone with the newest member of our family. Just recently arrived, Nell was an eleven month old border collie who had grown up in a kennel.

She was very serious and painfully well mannered. Xelie was ecstatic to have a young friend, and befuddled to discover that this newcomer didn't seem to understand or know how to play. Xelie made it her mission to make Nell feel welcome and bring her out of her shell.

Xelie would zoom about her reserved companion, play bowing then temptingly tossing toys all about. It took what seemed like an eternity to young Xelie, for her new friend to finally engage. You see Nell's upbringing had her convinced she would be considered a "bad dog" for anything other than perfect behavior.

But Xelie prevailed and it was then that their lifelong friendship began. Xelie was always generous with whatever she had, toys or otherwise. They played together, explored together and simply hung out. Xelie showed her that all of these things were "okay and good". She'd look out for and protect Nell if she sensed danger, especially if Lucy was anywhere nearby.

Xelie's best-friend, Nell.   *photo by Bob Degus*

Xelie had risen to alpha in her pack of two, her style and wisdom evident from the very start.

photo by Bob Degus

2.

A wooly wooly great job!

Before Xelie was even a twinkle in her mother's eye, Lucy had ruled the roost and, as I mentioned, she had inspired more than fear in her new home. In an effort to channel her intelligence to a more positive bent than Hitler-ic pack dominance, we decided and were determined to find something, other than another dog or person, that she could sink her teeth into.

Years prior we had taken our Newfie, Sprocket, for a fun day outing – a herding instinct test with some local trainers. We watched on as Sprocket raced joyfully after the sheep. He had a blast and so did we. Sadly Sprocket's body was less than suited to rigorous work. So thanks to a pair of dysplastic hips and a laundry list of other ailments, it was deemed sheep

Michele McGuire

photos by Bob Degus

Lucy on sheep.

6

herding was not in Sprocket's future.

But Lucy, she was a Shepherd mix after all. Shepherds, sheep, they go together, right? We scheduled an appointment. I'd love to recount a wonderful, relaxing, joyous occasion, but we were there with Lucy after all. And true to herself, she attempted to mount an attack on every other dog and person also awaiting their turn. Needless to say, we stood off to the side – waaaay off.

And then something happened. Lucy's eyes darted to the sheep as they turned a small group loose in a nearby pen. And for her, at this moment, the world stood still. All other dogs and humans, myself included, faded away. She stood there for several long seconds, utterly mesmerized. And then...

All hell broke loose. Lucy began pulling, lunging, barking and leaping – whatever those things were, she was uncontrollably drawn and compelled to make contact. I'm sure the average onlooker would have found the display frightening, or annoying, or both, but I was delighted. We had found something she was more interested in than canine world domination and bloodshed.

The moment of truth arrived none too quickly for Lucy. We attached a long line and then stepped through the gate and into the pen. The sheep took one look at this lunging beast and headed to the far fence. With a hint of apprehension, the instructor started toward his frightened flock, turned and faced Lucy and me, and told me to let go of the rope.

It was like loosing a lion onto a band of frightened Christians. Lucy charged straight toward the sheep. It was mayhem, dust flying, as they split and ran for their lives. I held my breath, hoping I wasn't about to witness sheepacide. Before long, the instructor miraculously had the sheep back in a group and Lucy circling about them. She'd go in for a nip now and then, but mostly she just wanted to work.

Now I was mesmerized. This was the most amazing thing I had ever seen. Before long, Lucy's sides were heaving and her dirt-covered tongue was three times its normal size. The man grabbed up the rope, reeled her in, and handed her back to me. "Not bad", he said.

It took all of my strength to pull Lucy out of the pen, away from those sheep. As I closed the gate behind us, the man called to his border collie who stood at attention. He began to whistle, and his dog, following every command, moved the sheep out of the pen and then brought out a new set.

It was at this instant my whole life changed. I wanted to do this as much as Lucy, maybe more.

We began scheduling regular lessons, several times a week. Lucy and I couldn't get enough. My husband was almost as enthused as I, so we quickly determined he needed a dog of his own to work.

Lucy was coming along beautifully, way above average for an upright dog. In layman's terms, that means she was fantastic for a non-Border Collie. Our aggression trainer had mentioned Lucy looked like a Picardy Shepherd. And upon some research, we discovered he was exactly right. We'd get a Picardy Shepherd and show those Border Collie people that other breeds could be just as good or better on sheep.

Xelie (right in green collar) and her brother traveling to America.   *photo by Bob Degus*

3.

Finding Xelie

La Valle du Mouton. When I heard the name of the kennel, I knew that was where we'd find our new puppy Picard. It was located in Innsbruck, Austria – just a small detail…

My husband made contact with the breeders and, lo and behold, they had a litter on the way. One hitch, they never shipped, and they never sold to people they hadn't met. There was a serious vetting process. If we wanted a puppy, we'd have to fly to Austria to meet them.

Thankfully the universe provided. My husband had run a significant amount of his workplace expenses through his American

Express. We had gobs of miles, without spending a dime of our own money. We had enough to fly first class from Los Angeles, California to Innsbruck, Austria. And that's exactly what we did.

Austrian Alps.   *cristians.ro/Moment/Getty Images*

The plan was this, we would spend three days visiting the puppies and getting to know the breeders. If at the end of the allotted time, we were deemed of sufficient caliber to be entrusted with one of these astounding creatures, then we would be allowed to write them a check and take it home.

In return, we asked that we be permitted to take the litter of puppies to a herd of sheep so we could discern which one was the most interested in livestock. Surprisingly, they agreed.

After a grueling and seemingly endless plane flight into Munich, followed by a lengthy railway trip south, we stepped off the train in Innsbruck. The Alps immediately enveloped us, majestic beyond all comprehension. A kindly looking man approached, hand extended; this was the breeder, Richard. We shook hands, meeting face to face for the very first time.

As we made our way to his car he explained "I've arranged for us to take the puppies to sheep". He opened the car door, revealing five rambunctious Picard puppies wrestling about in an enclosure in the back of his compact station wagon. He meant we were taking them right now. I was elated despite the heavy jet lag and exhaustion brought on by hours and hours of travel.

We had now been awake for almost twenty-one hours; and we were in a time zone completely opposite our own. And did I fail to mention, just before we left, we had sold our home and were in the middle of packing hell?

The excitement and anticipation I felt on the brink of finally moving to our gentleman's ranch, a full eight acres of herding heaven, was tainted by the fact that our mortgage broker, who was writing both a first and second loan on the property, had suddenly gone missing, refusing to answer any calls.

Contractually, we were bound to move one week from the day we were scheduled to return to L.A. Sane individuals might have surmised that perhaps it would be best to secure a new loan, rather than traverse the globe in pursuit of a puppy that we were in no way guaranteed to be granted.

But here we were, snaking our way up a narrow mountain road deeper and deeper into the Alps. Richard explained that the local shepherds had already moved their flocks into mountain pastureland for the summer. I kept spinning around in my seat, gazing at the rowdy band of pups, wondering which one was going to be ours.

Finally we arrived. As Richard stepped out of the car to greet the local farmer, I gazed at the pasture, lush and green, draped over a steep hillside; and in the distance, wooly silhouettes grazing peacefully in the sunlight. The moment of truth was almost here.

One by one, I took the puppies to see the sheep. Not an easy deal when you're nine thousand feet on the side of a mountain in pursuit of a creature that wants nothing to do with you or your dream. Needless to say, I did not lack for exercise that day.

The first puppy wriggled and snuggled but was not the least bit interested in the smell of lanolin or the fluff of wool. Same with the second and the third. What if none of the puppies showed any interest at all? How would we pick? How would we know?

Sheep in the Austrian Alps. *Federica Grassi / Moment Open / Getty Images*

The fourth puppy I reached for wore a thin green collar. You see they all had collars of different colors so the breeder could tell them apart. With a pinch of trepidation, I headed back into the pasture, back toward the flock.

This puppy felt different. She looked at me, then looked about, taking in her surround. And as her eyes scanned and surveyed the pasture, they eventually came to rest on a small group of nearby sheep. Her attention fixed, her body stiffened and grew still, and her nostrils pulsed rhythmically, almost imperceptibly, as she inhaled the scent.

She sees them. She's the first puppy who actually sees them. We stood there, motionless, for several eternal seconds as I watched her watch them. And then...

She went ballistic! This thoughtful, calm youngster exploded and was suddenly a wild beast, squirming, clawing, barking insistently, passionately. All she wanted was to get to those sheep. It took everything I had just to keep hold of her. Thank God for that little green collar, in more ways than one.

I took the final fifth puppy into the pasture, but as I made my way across the fresh spring grass, I knew, without a doubt, that the green collared female was the puppy for us.

Our new home after renovation.　　　　　　　　　　　　　　

photo by Bob Degus

4.

Careful what you wish for?

Xelie still wore her little green collar as we pulled up the gravel drive to our new home, or rather our new shack. The land was stunning, dotted with glorious old oak trees that stretched their resplendent branches over the front half of our brand new farm, indulging our drive in with soothing cool shade.

It had been a hellish week. Our mortgage broker had flaked and we some how, miraculously, had secured a first loan with our small credit union. But it had taken every financial asset we possessed, leaving us penniless. We needed the second loan to make the house habitable but, in order to be approved, nothing in our financial profile could change. That meant we could spend no money – not that we had any anymore...

We had planned to have the house cleaned and painted before we moved in. That did not happen. The house was in such a state that neither myself or my husband could bring ourselves to move any of our possessions inside. The moving truck arrived and we unloaded our material lives onto the wrap around porch and storage container we had recently purchased.

The Beverly Hillbillies would have felt right at home. "I'd live in a tent, to live on this land". That's what I said when we made the offer on our dream ranch. Careful what you wish for... Now here we were, about as close to a tent as we could get.

In the midst of this chaotic frightening crisis, I gazed at the dogs, frolicking in their new surround, breathing in all the luscious new scents, exploring all this space, this glorious space. They had no worries about the past or what was to take place in the future. They knew nothing of lost loans and financial woes.

The only thing that mattered to them was what was happening right now, and they were ecstatic. I glanced over at my husband, face drawn, exhausted, stress and anxiety twisting his features. At that moment, I would have given anything to be a dog...

Since we didn't have a tent, at least not one big enough to fit my husband, myself, my mom (who had come to help), plus our four dogs, and since we had no money to go to a hotel even if we could have found one that would take our entourage, we moved an old couch and one bed into the house for the night.

A small bit of moonlight trickled in through the windows, casting just enough light to reveal Lucy as she paced, going from window to window, peering outside. Now and again, she cocked her head to the side as the bone-chilling cries of a coyote kill nearby echoed through the canyon.

I believe this was the very first night my husband and I had chosen to sleep in separate quarters. The strain of the past two weeks had taken its toll. And although he loved the dogs and had been gung ho about trying his hand at herding with a pup of his own, the truth was, he was a city dweller, he loved the hustle, bustle and action of it all.

We had spent months restoring our beautiful 1930's Spanish home to utter perfection, when I announced I wanted to find some land and move. He had been a really good sport, supporting my dream, and agreeing to endeavor on another full home restoration, no small task coming right off the first one. The thought of spending an unknown amount of time living in a rodent infested hovel, with no means to make it habitable, had not been in the plan for either of us.

He was in the bedroom. I shared the couch with my mom. I could almost hear the Deliverance banjos dueling, as we wedged ourselves in opposite directions, our feet at each other's head. Xelie was not at all sleepy. She was like a manic alligator, chewing fiendishly on anything in her path. I had a giant supply of rawhides to protect myself and my flesh. My mother and I took shifts, passing the nine-week old beast back and forth, hoping and praying she'd finally fall asleep.

This is how our life with Xelie began. It was going to take faith and endurance to believe that all would work out. Up to this point, I guess my husband and I thought we were somehow untouchable, that we were in control of our destiny. Little did we know, we were about to step foot into a new era.

photo by Bob Degus

5.

Our new world

It took weeks, but we finally secured our second loan and began renovations. It was July 2001. The full summer heat had arrived and we were working with no air conditioning. Our small field was thriving in waist-high weeds of all kinds and I had allergies the likes of which I had never known.

"Why did you bring us to this God-forsaken place?" My husband's words played over and over in my mind. Even through the misery of my itchy watery eyes, I couldn't imagine a more beautiful little spot. The sun rose through the tangle of ancient oaks, casting artful shadows on the beginning of each day. It set over the mountains and hillside to the west, leaving behind the hours of long hard work, and painting the sky with a marvelous display of oranges, reds, magentas and more.

Xelie was a hellion or, rather, I should say a beautiful, independent, joyful being. She didn't have schedules or agendas and didn't understand why anyone else should. Every day was a wonder, filled with new experiences and adventure. She was always up for a playmate and never ready to end her day. That is a poetic way of saying, she was a major pain in the ass when you needed to get her inside for the night. "Catch me if you can" was one of her favorite puppy hood games. And at the end of a hot long day... Well, I think you get the picture.

Our Newfoundlands had been so compliant, always wanting to please. And Lucy was, well Lucy, but she had become very obedient as a result of our "professional help". So whose idea was it anyway to get this Picardy Shepherd?

By the end of August we had transformed our ramshackle dump into a quaint country cottage. It had been a long hard refurbishment, and our relationship and our marriage had suffered some major bumps and bruises. But now we were done. Now we could move forward with our lives. We commemorated the event with a beautiful candlelit dinner on our wonderful wrap-around porch.

I now had quality time for Xelie. Although I think she would have preferred that we all become feral and live off the land, she was happy to be getting more personal attention. My husband, who freelanced, was again back to work. And I was back to writing.

It wasn't long before I had sheep. It was heaven; I simply walked out my back door and could take Lucy to herd. Xelie was still too young and could only watch. She'd go crazy, barking and barking and barking and barking. Did I say she liked to bark? We had read somewhere that it was thought that two lines of Picards had survived the World Wars – a barking line and a quiet line. Gee, I wonder which one Xelie was from?

It seemed everything was back on track as August faded into September. It was early, just before seven in the morning, when the phone rang. We were about to get up anyway. My husband headed into the other room and answered. It was his mom. "No, I haven't been watching the..." his words trailed off as he gave me a funny look and headed to the television and turned it on. It was September 11, 2001. And as everyone knows, the world changed that day.

Even though the world had just been turned upside down, we still thought that we were somehow going to be immune to the aftermath of the 9-11 tragedy. And for a short time, that was so.

We were in the film business. It was all over the trades, fear running rampant that the resulting financial upheaval would affect investment in motion pictures. Prior to the catastrophe, there had been an average of seven hundred plus productions a year underway, both active and in development. Seven months post 9-11, that number had plummeted significantly below one hundred productions a year. Thankfully, my husband had just landed a sizeable gig that was slated to go into pre-production. Everything was going to be all right.

Xelie was now four months old, which my herding trainers informed me was old enough to start. I couldn't wait! Finally my husband and I were going to have something, other than work, that we could do together.

So together, we took her for her first official lesson on sheep. Xelie was on a flexi-leash as my husband took her into the pen or, to recount more accurately, as she took him in the pen. And for the next eight minutes, Xelie raced after the sheep, dragging my husband behind. Had he been a kite, he would have soared high above the unbridled display of pure energy and instinct.

As any stock-dog worth its salt would do, she went to the sheeps' heads and turned them, she'd cut back for any wooly that tried to escape, running, gathering, splitting the group, then re-gathering, over and over, until finally she tucked them neat and tidy into a corner where she held them, tongue to the ground. And none too soon as my husband gasped for air; he hadn't run like that in years.

Our instructors watched on, shocked and surprised; I don't believe they'd ever seen an upright dog so utterly keen for sheep. Xelie never stopped, from the time she started until the time she finished.

Xelie's first time on sheep

Success!

We drove home that day, glowing, overwhelmed with the promise our young pup showed. And Xelie smiled, as she poked her head out the car window, her wet beard blowing in the wind, looking back at the ranch -- she'd found her calling.

Teenage Xelie on sheep.   *photo by Bob Degus*

6.

To hunt or to herd?

As the next months passed and Xelie's training got underway, there was never a doubt about her zeal for sheep. The question simply became whether she wanted to work them or eat them?

I wish I'd known then what I know now. Xelie was much too young to start training. Had we known better, we would have waited until she was well beyond a yearling. Puppy brains are not yet fully developed. They need time to mature, both physically and mentally, especially for an activity such as herding.

You see, working livestock is very complex. It's basically a modified hunting instinct, utterly primal, calling back to the deepest most basic of genetic drives in both the dog and the sheep. It's not simply a learned behavior like obedience or agility. Dogs are driven to do things that even they don't understand.

It's about physics, based on the energy each creature emits. It's about predator and prey. It's a psychological chess game of who can outsmart who, which is the stronger, the quicker, and who is more clever. And ideally, in the end, after months and years of training, this game is handled by the human.

photo by Bob Degus

The bottom line? Xelie was extremely talented. She could work sheep with the best of them so long as they complied and were calm. But God help the ewe that was reactive or tried to escape. Xelie would give chase, pull it to the ground and...

Well, eating sheep is simply not allowed. It quickly became clear that Xelie was not the ideal dog for my husband to learn herding. He was also busy at work and my hours were much more flexible. We mutually agreed that I would put the basics on Xelie and then turn her over to him.

photo by Bob Degus

Working dogs was like a drug, I was addicted and I just couldn't get enough. A rather famous handler was coming to do a clinic at my trainer's facility, and I desperately wanted to go. The problem? They only worked with border collies. I had Lucy and Xelie, both great dogs, but...

Thankfully, a fellow student was empathetic and generous. She offered to let me borrow her dog. It was the first time I had worked a border collie and it was definitely different. The circus-act-lion-taming-chair-and-whip-like aspect was almost non-existent. I hadn't realized the amount of tension I'd been carrying when I worked Xelie and Lucy, or the amount of tension they carried when they came in contact with sheep.

To act like I had no part in facilitating anxiety in my dogs would be a lie. It was nothing I did on purpose, it was simply that I had no experience and was new to the whole process. Now, after years of training literally hundreds and hundreds of dogs, it's so clear there were many things I could have done differently. There were many foundations I could have laid to allow for more confidence and relaxation. What I wouldn't give to have young Xelie now.

My only consolation is to believe that everything happens for a reason. There was a reason she came into my life at the precise point in time that she did. And I wouldn't trade that for anything.

That said, the clinic was awesome. And in the end I was even more obsessed than I had been in the beginning. Someone made an off-handed comment that I may want to consider getting a border collie. The seed was planted.

Xelie and I continued to work and do battle. She had followed in Lucy's footsteps, earning several herding titles and ribbons. But the prey drive was still there and I always guarded for it.

My trainers made an offer – they had a young border collie for sale and asked if I'd like to try him. I sent the young dog around the sheep. He was amazing, keeping track of every minute movement the sheep made. He had "eye", something neither Lucy nor Xelie possessed being upright of style and breed. He just took care of things, without being asked.

I was any easy mark by now. You could have sold me a walrus if it worked sheep. I had my husband convinced that another dog would be no trouble. I was all set to buy this black and white prodigy when he suddenly disappeared. It's all hearsay, but I was told he had formerly been promised to someone else. They heard he was going to be sold, so quickly took possession.

Now, being a product of a consumer society, I had my taste buds set on a new border collie. The train was already rumbling down the track.

I was informed that the clinician who'd run the clinic I attended, had a number of border collies for sale. Problem? He lived in Virginia. Solution? My husband had continued to run business expenses through his Amex and, like before, we had plenty of miles for a free plane ticket. Compared to Innsbruck, Virginia was a piece of cake.

Suffice to say, I made the trip and returned with my selection. In the eye of the beholder, myself, she was a beautiful eleven-month old split faced red and white. In the eye of an unbiased observer, she was a matted, skinny wreck, with a crispy dry red coat. And she was an expensive wreck to boot. The only thing she knew how to do on sheep was flank and bring them. That's it. No brakes, no nothing. I didn't want a trained dog; I wanted to train one.

Up to that point, Xelie had attempted unsuccessfully to get my geriatric Newfoundlands to play. No matter how hard she tried, they were simply getting too old. And as I said, by now, she and Lucy were forever separated. My new little red and white Nell was the answer to Xelie's prayers.

Nell.

photo by Bob Degus

A moment of calm control, Xelie on sheep.   *photo by Bob Degus*

7.

Have ewe herd?

For the next year, not a day passed that I didn't work my dogs. They were all progressing. It had taken a bit to get hold of Nell, but she was working beautifully. Lucy's enthusiasm was waning a touch, but Xelie was still crazy about it. She could now gather the entire length of my trainer's three hundred yard field, unheard of for anything other than a border collie or kelpie. Did I mention I had to sprint the length of the field and meet her at the other end to ensure the sheep's safety? Thank God I'd been a distance runner since my teens.

In any event, the training facility was gearing up to hold a trial sanctioned by the USBCHA (United States Border Collie Handler's

Association). A border collie field trial, the most difficult venue, I'd come to learn. Everyone encouraged me to enter.

I hadn't gotten into herding to compete; I had been spellbound by the work itself, and training process alone. But my dogs were doing so well I thought, what the hell, I'll try it. I entered Nell in the Nursery, an advanced class for young dogs, and Xelie in the novice, knowing she'd probably be the only non-border collie at the trial. Sadly, Lucy didn't have a gather long enough to compete.

I now had my work cut out for me – Xelie would have to do a one hundred-plus yard outrun from my side, and I couldn't leave the spot I sent her from. She'd be gathering without me there to protect the sheep. God help us!

We practiced, and practiced, and practiced, and then the day came.

Nell's class ran before Xelie's. Nell was phenomenal, placing second her first trial ever. Before long, Xelie and I walked to the post. Heart pounding, I sent her. She ran out, got about half way, then stopped...

And took a dump. It seemed like forever. A physiologic necessity or a symbolic statement? I'm sure the sight brought great pleasure to another student with whom I'd had a falling out. I knew what Xelie could do -- and this was just shit.

I'm sure Xelie could feel my disappointment as we made the drive home.

The following day, Nell again excelled. My heart was pounding even louder this time as I approached the post with Xelie for her second and last chance in this trial. It was a lot to ask of a non-border collie breed. But I knew if Xelie tried, if she could get her head around it, it would be a walk in the park, so to speak...

I sent her. The trajectory she took was perfect. Her scruffy wheaten hair rustled lightly in the wind as she stretched out reaching her maximum speed, stride powerful, graceful, and confident. She came in behind her small band of sheep, lifted them beautifully and marched them straight down the field to my feet. Expertly, she held them to me as we made our way around the course like seasoned professionals, then arriving at the pen, she masterfully convinced them to walk calmly in so I could close the gate. She beamed up at me, thoroughly pleased with herself. I could imagine her saying, "Now can I eat them?"

Xelie, a Picardy Shepherd, an upright breed, a non-border collie, took first place at a border collie trial. I didn't know if it had ever been done. It was Xelie's proudest herding moment. The dream had become reality, at least on this day. It had taken a lot of hard work on both my part and Xelie's, but we'd done it.

Xelie winning first place at a border collie trial.   *photo by Bob Degus*

When we got back home, I proudly hung her blue ribbon from her collar and sent her into the house to tell my husband all about it. It is still, even now, one of the most amazing competitive moments I've ever shared with a canine working partner.

Xelie's AHBA qualifying titles.
photo by Bob Degus

photo by Bob Degus

8.

Going to the dark side

I now had a taste of competition and was surprised to discover I liked it, I really did. What was it about the adrenaline pumping uncontrollably through my veins, the nausea, the loss of appetite and endless trips to the Porta-Potty that I found so attractive?

I hadn't competed at anything since I was a kid and now, in my early forties, here I was chomping at the bit to go to another trial. I knew I could take Nell, and I wanted to take Xelie but... Was she reliable? Could I take her to a new place, on sheep she didn't know, and have everyone survive? It wasn't a joke; it was a serious consideration.

32

I'm sure Xelie didn't understand when I took off for the next competition without her. I wish she and I could have just reached some agreement, a peace treaty of sorts, where I could have done something for her and, in exchange, she would have agreed to never take down another sheep. I just didn't know what that something was. And neither did she... Or if she did, she wasn't talking.

I was getting in deeper and deeper. I had now taken on a couple of projects, border collies with major issues. I worked and tried things on my own, attempting to fix them. Before long, one of the projects was living with us. And I had a second dog to trial. His name was Mick.

I still continued to work Xelie but, I sadly admit, my dream with her was fading. It had become clear my husband was not going to find the time to work her and, even if he had, she would never have suited a beginner. Since Picards were not yet eligible for AKC trials, I had considered taking her to one other border collie trial, but had chickened out at the last minute as our practices were still at times subject to bloodshed.

We had wanted to breed Xelie and introduce Picards to the American herding community. But as her prey drive persisted, I began to have doubts. A questionable hip x-ray sealed Xelie's fate; she would never be a mother. And what an amazing mother she would have been.

So as I went to trial after trial, Xelie was left behind. I couldn't even take her along for the ride. You see, at dog trials, sheep are often moved in the midst of dogs, many times when you least expect it. I couldn't take the chance Xelie would get loose and onto someone else's sheep. And there was the barking...

It makes me weep to think of it now, leaving her at home. What a waste, what a horrible waste.

By July of 2003, our financial situation was less than ideal and my husband could find no work. No matter how much I wrote or how hard I tried, I couldn't get a bite on any of my scripts. Our cash flow was minimal and we'd begun living on credit.

But somehow we still believed that this was only temporary. I took off to New Mexico, traveling out off state to compete for the very first time. No money, no work, but there was a dog trial, so I had to go. That's how addicted I'd become.

It was there in New Mexico I found my next pup, a freckle spattered tri-color female I named Molly. Have I told you what a good sport my husband had been? We had all of $500 to our name when I asked to spend $300 on Molly. He said yes. Unbelievable... Unbelievable that I would ask; unbelievable he would agree.

Molly   *photo by Bob Degus*

We had never been a practical pair, my husband and I, that's probably how we landed in the business we were in. We believed in being true to yourself and following your dreams. We both knew how to work hard, eighty hour work weeks were not at all unusual. We tried to be smart about it, but when there came a choice between practicality and a life long quest, we always followed the same path...

Nell was now qualified for the National Finals. We both agreed I would take her to Sturgis and run her in the Nursery class. It was an exciting trip and Nell did well, placing 22nd out of 150 dogs. Our first trial year, our first Nationals. Broke as we were, my husband was very proud.

Molly had been a joy, keenly watching every run that she could. We'd happened into her brother who was in need of a home. And well, I'm sure you can guess what happened next. No, I didn't spend our last dime; I bartered some future training on a dog of their choice, in exchange for the pup.

Xelie was happy when we all returned home. She was especially happy to see Nell, her very best friend and confidant. This was the longest they'd ever been apart. She greeted our new member, Molly's brother, Buddy, who'd found his new home.

Xelie's pack had grown to five. There was Nell, Molly, Mick, Buddy, and of course Xelie herself. We still had Lucy, but she was her own pack of one, isolated from the others.

Despite the growing numbers, Xelie's leadership style remained as it had always been, fair and caring. Peace, play and harmony prevailed in our pack, at least among the dogs.

Xelie and the author, Michele McGuire.

photo by Bob Degus

9.

My turn

The mounting financial stress was reaching a breaking point – something had to give. We were getting deeper and deeper into debt, and the conventional methods we had always employed were no longer yielding work.

My husband came up with an idea – create a micro-budget film company of our own. He drew up a business plan that spanned the making and selling of at least three of these pictures.

I wrote a script for the first maiden production, a script crafted so that we could shoot for next to no money, using our ranchette as the sole location. We scheduled and budgeted and, calling in favors we had accumulated over the years, came up with a number, a proposed cost, for the first picture.

To be a film director had been my husband's dream since I met him. I'd always supported this pursuit, but becoming a film director in Hollywood without familial or star-studded connections was a challenge even more difficult than either of us had anticipated.

We had grunted our way through the production ranks, rising to Line Producer and Producers, both of us. We had both been nominated for Academy Awards and Ace Awards. The terms of our new company were that my husband would direct the script that I had written, and I would be the Producer.

Amazingly, within months, my husband found investors. A friend he had known from college. He and his partner loved my script and, before long, we had money for pre-production, allowing a minimal salary for both of us, just enough to tourniquet our hemorrhaging debt.

I was no stranger to the nuts and bolts of movie making; I knew how many hats I was going to have to wear on a micro budget like this. I knew the tremendous hours that were in store – an eighty-hour work-week was going to be a vacation in comparison.

When would I have time to work my dogs, much less take weekends off to compete with them?

Have I mentioned what an incredibly good sport my husband had been in the pursuit of my herding addiction? He had also been incredibly supportive of my writing dream.

It was my turn now, to support his aspiration with all the energy I had. Working dogs would just have to wait.

Well, almost… I had written sheep and a working dog into the script. Nell became a star. The camera crew was dazzled by how I could get her to hit her mark every time when we filmed sheep work. These are my fondest memories of the actual production period.

The making of our movie was an experience of extremes.

Our home was the sole location. All of our belongings had been removed. It had been painted and set dressed to look like a rundown dive. Hell, we should have shot there before we renovated! A back room was our production office.

Nell and the author, Michele McGuire on the film set.   *photo by Jon Silberg*

Again, I needed a tent. I borrowed my friend's small travel trailer instead. Ever supportive, my mother had come to help, taking care of my dogs so they wouldn't feel abandoned. She, my husband, and I moved into the tiny trailer several days before cameras actually rolled.

To say pre-production had been demanding would be an understatement, but at least my husband and I were still on the same page, we were a team. But by the end of the first day of actual filming, it became clear that our partnership was going to remain only in my memory.

My husband left the travel trailer and took up residence in our movie set, what used to be our bedroom.

This is not the place to go into detail, suffice to say at the end of our twenty-five day shoot, my husband and I weren't speaking to each other. Well, unless it was necessary for business…

We had worked together since the day we met; in fact, we met at work. We had always gotten along. It was tragic. At the culmination of ten plus years of persistence and hard work, here we stood, both realizing our dream – his to direct a feature film and mine to get a feature script made. And after all this, the chasm between us was so vast, we couldn't even raise a glass to one another in a toast.

Again, careful what you wish for, I guess… On the one hand, after nine months of gut-wrenching labor, the final product was born, and it was outstanding, especially for a picture made on a shoestring, or more accurately, a tidbit of a shoestring.

On the other hand, was it worth detonating and blasting our relationship into the netherworld?

Looking back, I think we were both compelled to follow the paths we did. I guess everything happens for a reason.

After the dust settled and we had several successful screenings, we began an attempt to pick up the pieces. In December of 2004, our financiers and business partners announced a slight change in the business plan. They wanted to try to sell the movie we had just made BEFORE beginning on the second picture.

This had not been the original plan. If it had, my husband and I would have budgeted a higher salary for ourselves to see us through this period. Suffice to say, whether we liked it or not, we went on hiatus.

We thought the stress was extreme prior to creating the little company. We were back in the financial hole that we had been in previously, only now, we didn't have each other, not really.

As the months drew on and things got even uglier, I'd take refuge in working my dogs. One cannot run a dog on sheep without being in the present, in the moment. And when you're in the moment, all the disasters and fears for the future disappear.

We were closing in on bankruptcy when, in the spring of 2005, a friend asked if I would be interested in teaching herding at a local agility facility. I'd already been helping a few people here and there, and we needed the money.

Before long, I was working full time, teaching at the facility and in my own back yard. The income was bridging the gap, well almost... My herding addiction was now a necessity on a number of levels, practical, financial, emotional and psychological.

Somehow that year, I got all three of my dogs qualified for the National Finals -- Nell in the Open, and Buddy and Molly in the Nursery. And Xelie was still working, in my field on hand-picked sheep that she wouldn't attack.

I'm sure Xelie would have liked to work more than she did, but she also loved being outdoors, in the country, with all that implies. She had a good life, certainly better than the average city dweller.

As for the film business? I was tired of chasing the carrot. I just couldn't continue in the belief that everything was going to be all right, that we'd somehow break through to the other side and be outrageously successful as writer and director, especially given the cautious post 9-11 environment. I didn't have anything more to prove, I knew I was a good writer and I knew I was an exemplary filmmaker, I knew it in my heart. I'd also seen the underbelly of greedy, dishonest power seekers, I'd seen them over and over in this business. I was done, just done.

I could be happy making a living training stock dogs. Everything happens for a reason, right? Maybe that's why Lucy came into my life? And Xelie, and Nell and... Well, you know the cast of characters.

I began working on a business plan of my own, researching what areas of the country would suit this endeavor and afford me plenty of opportunity to compete in dog trials. I'd narrowed it down to Texas, Virginia, Pennsylvania and maybe New York.

Even though our relationship was strained, my husband was on board. I could tell he felt defeated and was fighting inner demons. But what were our choices, what were they really? We couldn't find work, and property the likes of which I would need to continue a herding business, was not within our financial reach. We agreed that if by summer's end the movie hadn't sold, we'd sell our home and get out of California.

The end of August came and went and nothing had changed. We interviewed a successful local real estate agent and put our dream ranchette on the market. Again, I headed off to the National Finals waving farewell to Xelie and my husband...

And before I returned, our home was sold. I had been on the internet researching properties before I made the trip, so my husband and I already had a good idea where we were going, and what we were going to look at, when I got home.

We went to Pennsylvania -- too expensive. Virginia – one possibility. We'd ruled out upstate New York because of the winters. Our last stop was Texas. I'd spent much of my childhood in Texas and, although I hadn't lived there in twenty-five years, when I stepped off the plane there I somehow felt at home.

I had chosen the Austin area, centrally located with lots of agility facilities from which to draw my initial business. My mom, who was now living alone and approaching her eighties, lived less than two hours away. If she ever needed anything, I'd be nearby to help.

As we made our way down a narrow tree-lined country road leading to our first contender, I remember thinking how much I'd love to live off a beautiful little road like this...

The house was cute and in need of absolutely NO work. It sat atop a small hillside, dotted with stunning mature oaks. The field was smaller than I'd wanted, but the layout was good for working dogs.

After three days of looking at countless properties, that cute little country road we'd driven down the very first day, would be the road that led to our new home and...

Country road leading to our new home.

photo by Bob Degus

10.

A new start

I was excited about starting on a new venture, about working for myself and being in charge of my own success or failure. My triumph, or lack thereof, would no longer be subject to someone else's taste, or agenda, or what favors I could or could not provide. The dogs I trained would either be able to work or they wouldn't and my success would be based on that. I felt confident.

Again, in retrospect, to an outsider, it sounds crazy. I was changing careers in my mid forties, was moving halfway across the country to a place where I knew no one, to open a sheep herding business. Really?

Xelie and my ever growing pack of canine friends were all for it. More space, more sheep, more herding? Made perfect sense to them.

I kept asking my husband if he was okay with the prospect? What was he going to do? I never got a clear answer. When I look back, I think I was running toward a fresh beginning and he was running away from his perceived failure.

Sadly, the joy and anticipation I felt about starting anew was gravely interrupted in the weeks to come. It had an eerily similar emotional flavor to the move we made out of the city in 2001. Only this time the strain was not a financial one.

Shortly after we returned home, our offer having been accepted on our new Texas ranch, my young horse Squeak foundered and became seriously compromised. "If you move him, you'll kill him" the vet had explained.

Squeak   *photo by Bob Degus*

So as we packed and prepared to move, I scrambled to find an arrangement where Squeak could be treated and cared for until he was well enough to make the trip. One of my herding clients was an answer from God. Her husband was a farrier and had worked on Squeak's feet, and she

44

was a long-time equestrian in charge of a barn filled with multi-million dollar horses. They had a friend with a small place and an empty stall. They would look after Squeak.

We were less than a week from closing on the new house and moving, when another tragedy befell us. Five months prior, Xelie had welcomed Annie, a beautiful blue, six-month old border collie, into our group. She had shown noteworthy herding promise and had quickly become one of Xelie's favorite companions, next to Nell of course.

Annie idolized Xelie and followed her everywhere. They shared an independent spirit and liked to explore together, while the others were content to remain close to the house.

It was twilight when I finished giving my last lesson. It had been a long day and I'd been working since 8 a.m. I was starved; I hadn't eaten. My client asked if I'd like her to padlock the gate behind her on her way out.

Annie

And when she was gone I let the dogs out and went in to eat. She had not closed the gate tightly. Annie got out and was hit by a car. She was still alive when I found her. Xelie was in a panic, leaping in and out of my truck as we loaded the injured dog to take her to the vet. I have never before, or since, seen Xelie so upset.

Four days and thousands of dollars later, Annie became septic and died. Perhaps Xelie blamed herself for teaching the young dog to wander? Perhaps that's why she was so distraught? Her vocation had always been to care for and protect those she loved.

I definitely blamed myself for not double-checking the gate before I let the dogs out. And Annie was in my mind, ever present in my mind. Every time I closed my eyes there she was. She didn't understand what had happened. She was happily frolicking with the pack at one moment, then forever separated the next.

I was inconsolable and so was she.

As our plane took off from L.A. headed to our closing in Austin, I couldn't keep from crying. The grief and shock were so overwhelming I didn't care who saw my tears.

I closed my eyes and prayed for help. In my mind' s eye, Annie was there, as always, looking lost, confused and upset. Before long, a friend who had passed away two years prior, approached. Her name was Carla, a fellow animal lover.

I had been with Carla for the final three days of her life; I had been with her when she drew her last breath and passed. The experience had been profound, and left me with no doubt that there is a world beyond death where our spirits dwell until whatever comes next – or not, depending on your beliefs.

And now here was Carla, at thirty thousand feet, in my mind. Her look was comforting. She approached Annie and smiled, then picked her up and held her in her arms. She looked back at me as if to say, "Everything is going to be okay. I'll take care of her".

After a moment, she turned and started back the way she came, taking Annie with her. Annie draped her head over Carla's shoulder and looked back at me as they walked away. And when they were gone from sight, I knew Annie was going to be all right.

From that point forward, when I closed my eyes, Annie was no longer there. She had moved on.

Annie's was not the first death of a beloved animal friend that I'd experienced. I'd lost Sprocket and Dot two years before. But they were older, they'd lived their lives, they were ready to pass. And shortly after they'd gone, they each, in their own way, returned to say their farewell with a symbolic gesture they knew I'd recognize.

Annie was different, she was in shock, she'd only just begun her life. She didn't know what had happened or how to move on. To this day I thank Carla for her help.

So as I made the trips back and forth between California and Texas, moving my sheep in two separate groups, I drove with grief still trickling down my cheeks. Six days later, by the light of a marvelous full moon, I pulled my truck and trailer down the driveway to our new home.

The dogs were happy to stretch their legs after hours of confinement. I watched as they frolicked in the moonlight, sniffing, playing, and racing about. We'd reached our destination and it was time for a new start.

photo by Bob Degus

11.

I couldn't say no...

Just before our moving truck headed out of California, my husband's spirits finally lifted. He had found an agent who wanted to represent him as a Director. He was ecstatic and hopeful once again.

Although I was delighted for him, I wasn't sure how this was going to work now that we were about to live in Texas. It was simple, he informed me, he'd keep an apartment in L.A.

Now we had made a profit on our ranchette, having sold just weeks before the real estate market crashed. We'd walked away being able to pay off our debts, purchase our new home and have a tiny bit of cushion left over.

Months before, he had told me he was done with the film business but I knew deep in my heart that wasn't so; filmmaking was all he had, all he'd ever known or been interested in for his entire adult life. Sheep herding had been a passing fancy; directing was his passion.

True to form, I couldn't say no. This was his dream, after all. So my husband helped move our belongings into the new twenty-acre paradise, then left a week later, going back to L.A.

Here I was out in the middle of nowhere, in a place where I knew no one, about to embark on a business that was unconventional at best. It's amazing how a dream can seduce you into a euphoric state of optimism, in spite of the odds.

Being a writer, I was no stranger to spending time alone. Besides, I had my dogs and now, while I was preparing the property to open for business, I actually had as much time as I had always wanted to spend with them.

photo by Bob Degus

There was land to clear, fences and pens to erect and business to drum up. Thankfully I was able to hire out the hard labor. In the two months it took to complete the facility, I played with my dogs, I worked them on sheep, I had long talks and walks with them. And we simply hung out. I was more a member of the pack than I had ever been. I was living more in the present than ever before. Believe it or not, it seemed like the first stress-free time I'd had in years.

My husband would come to visit every two to three weeks. Maybe everything, both business and personal, would now begin to recover.

My first clients were local agility instructors whom I had invited out for a free lesson and look at my new herding center. In return, I had asked if they liked what they saw, that they refer me to others.

This is how my business began, and before long I was working full time.

photo by Bob Degus

12.

The beginning of the end

As anyone who runs their own business soon discovers, there is no such thing as a true day off, especially when your business is in your own back yard, literally. I was open for lessons five-days a week and I trained dogs, both my own and those belonging to clients, seven days a week.

But despite all the hours, it hardly seemed like work. I loved the sport, and was passionate about teaching and training. I loved to be outdoors, I loved dogs and most of the people I had met so far were quite delightful. My business was thriving....

My husband's was not. He remained enmeshed in the same

51

horrendous struggle we had been in prior to the move. Dealings with our business partners were becoming more and more bizarre and it was beginning to look like our movie was never going to be sold.

My husband and I were now traveling down separate roads – mine led to the ever-present mind-set of the dog world, his traversed the slippery slopes of filmmaking hell. My dream of writing was growing faint, his dream of directing seemed almost insurmountable.

These were very dark times for him. And perhaps had I been more inspired, I somehow might have been able to make a difference. I simply didn't know how to crack the filmmaking nut; if I had, I would have done it years ago.

Again, I was done with the movie business – but my husband was not. By 2008, we finalized our divorce.

I was now completely on my own. Well, not entirely, I had my beloved dogs, and Xelie managed the ever-growing pack with her usual panache. And thank God she did, as I was now putting in an easy 12-14 hour workday.

It was around this time I declared Xelie fully retired. There had been several unfortunate mishaps and she was now seven years old. If I hadn't been successful exorcizing the prey drive by now, what made me think anything was going to be different in the future?

It was a gradual retirement. As I got busier and busier, she got worked less and less. I was too busy to notice whether or not she noticed. How sad is that?

I'd say everything must happen for a reason, but what possible reason could there be for failing to notice or listen to the heart and soul of one of the most amazing spirits I have ever known?

As always, Xelie was an exemplary example, she somehow forgave me and continued on living moment by moment, being the best Xelie she could be, leading my pack into daily peace and harmony.

But day after day as I worked dogs on sheep down in the field,

Xelie's voice would ring out from the upstairs bedroom where she spent much of her time, crying out for another opportunity to work sheep herself.

Xelie in upstairs window.

I'd see her face in the window, looking out at the activity below. And that was all I'd see, her cute little face. I completely missed the plea for a second or third or fourth chance. Just any chance to work the flock once again.

photo by Bob Degus

13.

The lost years

The cushion my husband and I had been blessed with when we sold our California ranchette had been completely gone for some time now. I was making enough money to stay afloat but not get ahead.

So I increased my workload, hard to believe that was possible. I started traveling to out of town facilities to give clinics and lessons. And my income increased. But every time I started to get ahead, some catastrophe would whisk away the surplus I'd just gathered. This happened over, and over, and over, and over.

A theme was developing, even a blind man could see. The

universe was trying to tell me something, and it wasn't that I was going to be rich beyond all imagination, at least not rich in the material sense of the word.

I surmised I was going to need to learn to trust that if I continued to work hard, the universe would provide. Not an easy pill for a control freak to swallow. But I wasn't willing to give up the business I had worked so hard to build, and there was nothing else I could imagine or find the desire to do.

I was getting tired, but there were still so many things I loved about what I did. So day in and day out, for the next six years, I put my nose to the grindstone, and worked and worked and worked.

And the longer I worked, the less I became truly connected to my dogs and their emotional world. The numbers had grown. They were well cared for physically, but I barely had the energy to crawl into bed each night, much less spend the time it would take to make each one feel special. Horrible, I know.

They were my co-workers during the week and my partners to compete with at trial events. I loved them, of course, but they'd become more like members of my staff than intimate friends.

To say I was a workaholic who had nothing but work would be redundant, but painfully true in my case. Thankfully, I had found a breed, the border collie, that was my equal in this department.

Do you know a male border collie will pass by a bitch in standing heat, if given the choice between stock work and sex? And I thought I was extreme. All that's to say, I'm sure the border collies took my preoccupation with endlessly laboring for survival much more in stride than the forgotten Xelie.

Somehow Xelie's zest for life remained intact. She'd still leap in the air excitedly when she was about to go outside. She'd give me a friendly poke right in the buttocks with her scruffy nose every morning and evening on a daily basis. I thought it was a sign of affection, but maybe she was trying to tell me something. Let's see, a poke in the butt... Was she telling me I was being an ass, from the beginning of the day to the end?

If so, from where I sit at this moment, I'd say she was completely right. It's so frightfully easy to get caught up in the minutiae of it all. The broken this, the falling apart that, the how will I pay for this, how will I do that? And by now minutiae was my middle name.

The house was like a fair skinned woman who'd been out in the sun much too long – it had aged, and not at all well. The list of needed repairs was growing longer and longer. And the means with which to fix them simply did not exist.

Today as I write, I think of these as the lost years. The years lost to worry. The years lost to blind obsessive work. The years lost, that could have been spent loving and caring for my dogs the way Xelie always cared for them. The lost years that Xelie could have indulged in her passion; the years lost that she could have been herding.

The lost years; the years I'd lost sight of what was truly important. If I'm honest, much of my life should be entitled the lost years.

Muriel McGuire

14.

Please, stop the merry go round!

On December 24th, 2012, my work world stopped for the first time in seven years. It was early evening; my dad, stepmother and brother were visiting for the holidays from out of town, when the phone rang. I almost didn't hear it.

My mother was in the emergency room; she'd had a serious stroke. Our Christmas Eve party quickly came to an end as we raced to the hospital two hours away. I had given the okay to a drug, that had risks to be sure, but that was my mother's only chance at a somewhat normal recovery. There was, essentially, a 30% chance she would not survive, with or without it.

My mother had been my rock. At eighty-four years old, just weeks prior, she'd been taking care of my place, my sheep, and at least eight or nine dogs, while I was away giving lessons at a facility in Houston. Since I had moved to Texas, she had been my official ranch caretaker when I was away on business or at a dog trial.

My dogs loved her and she loved them. I think over the lost years, she supplied them the emotional connection that I was too work-bound to give. She had always supported me in my endeavors, and been helpful whenever she could. She was my number one, very best, most amazing friend and confidant.

When we chose Austin as our new home, I told myself I was there, in part, to be available to her should she need any help in her later years. The reality was that, since I had moved to Texas, she had been much more helpful to me than I ever dreamed of being to her.

And there she lay, in ICU, struggling for her very survival. I had always, effectively, lived in denial that she was getting older and that very possibly the day would come when our relationship would change, or end, on this plane anyway. But here we stood on the precipice of the inevitable.

The drug seemed to be working. She was now conscious and had regained use of her right arm and right leg. She couldn't communicate very well, but she could clearly understand what the doctors were asking her to do.

The hospital staff seemed encouraged. I did not want to leave my mom alone. My brother and his son were still at my house awaiting an update. He was kind enough to agree to look after the dogs for the night.

My dad's flight took off the following day. My brother picked me up from the hospital and returned me to my home so I could pick up my truck and have transportation back and forth.

My usual pet-sitter was already overbooked for the holidays. Thankfully, after two days of driving back and forth caring for my mom on one end, and the dogs on the other, she organized a small group of my students to take shifts caring for my pack. It was incredibly thoughtful and generous on everyone's part as most of these people had to travel at least an hour, one-way, just to reach my house.

I now could concentrate solely on being a support and advocate for my mom. You see, within the first forty-eight hours, she'd suffered at least one, possibly two additional strokes. You could only use the miracle drug once, and we'd already used it the first night.

By day three, my beautiful mother could no longer move her right arm. She could barely move her right leg. She couldn't speak, or swallow, and she could barely move. More than once I feared she wasn't going to make it at all.

My mom had been a devout Catholic, Christian in a genuine way. She lived her faith without being judgmental about others, and she mostly didn't shove her beliefs down anyone's throat – every now and then she'd try to get me to sample a taste, hoping I'd like it, but her love was never contingent on whether I, or anyone else, believed as she did.

I mention this now because of what happened the first night in ICU. She was conscious and awake. I asked if she'd like to watch television? She nodded. I found WTN, the religious channel she had always watched regularly. She shook her head, wanting me to turn to another station. I was shocked, but complied.

I surfed the channels, waiting for her to give me a nod when we came across something she wanted to watch. Finally, after passing over countless shows, she nodded as enthusiastically as one can, who has just had a stroke.

It was a Barbara Stanwick movie; in fact as it turned out, it was a Barbara Stanwick marathon. And for those of you who remember Barbara, she was the quintessential strong, independent woman of an era gone by when men's and women's roles were more traditional. The characters she played were, for the most part, ahead of their time. I should have known then, when my mother watched back-to-back Stanwick, that she had no intention of giving up.

For almost two weeks I slept in a chair beside my mother's bed, spending day and night with her. I got updates how the dogs were doing, but I never went home. The incessant obsession with my job had finally ceased; for the first time in seven years there was something more important than work. In retrospect, I think my mother's stroke was my first wake-up call.

It was now mid January 2013; she had finally stabilized enough to be moved to a rehabilitation center. She still couldn't eat, move, or use the restroom. Completely helpless, she was going to have to start over from the very beginning.

The facility in Austin was lovely, close enough that I could see her each day. She began to improve with the help of her therapists. And I began to work again, half days so I could visit in the afternoons.

I think the most difficult part of this whole process was the fact that my mom could no longer communicate; her language center had been obliterated. Gone were those in depth conversations we used to enjoy. Gone were the inside jokes, the playful kidding around, the interaction that we'd both so cherished.

No one could give me a prognosis. "All strokes are different", they'd say, adding that there's a distinct window of time for improvement. The initial three to four months are crucial, then additional improvement can occur up to a year post stroke but, beyond that, improvement plateaus and levels out.

The dogs were happy to have me back, even if it was part time. For the next three weeks, I split my time between my work and my visits to rehab. Again, as before with the dogs, even though I was there physically, I was not fully there emotionally. I was preoccupied with the future; something they weren't built to understand.

It was becoming clear that my mother's recovery would be slow, regardless of how hard she was working. Insurance was dictating the end of rehab; my mother would have to move. The choices were a nursing home, or my home.

Muriel, in rehab, her friend Bob and Lucy.

As much as I wanted to help in my mom's recovery, I must admit I was overwhelmed. The task was daunting; she still could hardly move. She couldn't get out of bed and into her wheelchair without the assist of a full transfer, much less go to the bathroom, or take a shower, or simply sit on the couch to watch TV. She'd only just graduated to pureed foods and the peg-tube remained as a backup feeding system. Her continence was still unreliable. I couldn't believe this was the insurance company's definition of rehabilitated. But it was.

There was no way my beloved mother was going to rot in a stinking nursing home, so overwhelmed or not, I was going to have to learn some new skills so I could bring her to live in my home safely. For thirty years I had invited my mom to come live with me or, at least, live in the same city as me. It took a paralyzing stroke to get her to agree, that's how independent she was.

I learned how to transfer her into a wheelchair, a car, a bed, whatever she needed. I learned what foods she could eat and how to prepare them, I learned her medications and the schedule she was on, and many other things that I won't mention. And then the day came that I brought her home.

On their own, Xelie's in charge   *photo by Bob Degus*

I was as confident as I could be without being confident at all. I transferred her successfully into the car, loaded her wheelchair and her bags, and took off for home.

Now I will spare you the details of the weeks and months to follow, suffice to say it was a challenge the likes of which I had never known. It became clear my days of travel for business and dog trials were a thing of the past. Leaving my mother alone was out of the question, and there were no financial resources for any outside help.

As for the dogs, they were now getting next to no personal attention from me. They were on their own, in their pack, with the amazing Xelie as their leader. And amazing she was, as peace and harmony prevailed as it always had under her rule.

photo by Bob Degus

15.

Did I tell you I was a dog trainer?

I wanted more than anything for my mother to recover, both for her and for me. From the beginning I had researched and tried to figure out how to help facilitate the process.

Home Health had begun and she now had three therapists visiting at various times during the week. But it wasn't enough. She needed to practice what they were teaching her. Remember, we had a window of time; the more she could regain within this period, the more fully she would recover.

Sadly, the stroke had taken more than my mother's ability to speak, or the use of her right side. Stealthily, it had also robbed her of the ability to initiate activity on her own.

If she was going to improve, I was going to have to take charge of her practice and strength building.

It occurred to me that rehabilitating my mom wasn't all that different from training a dog. Yes, she was a human, but... Define the problem, build the foundations and lock in the behavior with plenty of repetition. It would take work, but I knew how to do that.

I would train dogs in the morning and my mother in the afternoon. I'm sure she was thrilled. Yeah, right...

As anyone eligible for AARP knows, when the roles reverse and it becomes time for the child to care for the parent, there are countless invitations for sadness, conflict and struggles. My mother and I were not immune, despite the amazing relationship she and I had shared over the years.

The first couple months as she made notable gains, we worked together as a team. But as the months drew on, and progress began to wane, so did my mother's fighting spirit. She had worked so hard, yet even the most basic of things remained difficult. She now could stand and walk a little, supporting herself on a countertop. But unless she faithfully did her exercises, the stroke would again take charge and she would weaken. I think, for her, it was very demoralizing.

I held on and persevered. Basically, I became a Commandant. I began using tough love. If I'd had a crate, she'd have been in lockdown. For those of you that know me, you know what I mean.

For the first time in over thirty years, my mother and I began to argue as I attempted to force my will on her life. I wanted her to get well and time was running out. But so was my mother's desire to try. She'd been an incredible inspiration, a role model for acceptance, endurance and hard work up to now. I just wouldn't take no for an answer. I was so caught up in my own wants, that I had lost sight of hers.

I had overlooked one very important detail, an aspect essential to training herding dogs. At the end of the day, no matter how much pressure I applied to gain a specific behavior, the dog got to do something it loved; they got to work the sheep. And almost invariably, whatever aspect I'd been training, would help them be more successful than they had been before, making the final experience even more pleasurable. They got a reward.

Where was the reward for my mother? She worked and worked and worked and the gains she made could be lost at the drop of a hat. She'd been a healthy independent woman up until the stroke. Her reward would have been to regain her faculties and her independence. It was clear eight months post-stroke, this was not going to happen short of a miracle.

Muriel on ATV.

It was late August of 2013 when my mother declared that she wanted to sell her home. It was a landmark; an admission and resignation to the fact that she would never be able to return home and live independently as before. None of us had wanted to admit it, but we were now almost nine months into the stroke and we couldn't deny that she was correct.

The insurance company had stopped paying for home health and there were no longer visits from outside therapists. The overhead associated with maintaining her home devoured all her financial assets, making private care impossible.

In early October, my mother signed the documents closing on the sale of her home. It was her birthday. Surprisingly, she was not at all sad about leaving her former life behind. She remained an example, as she had always been. She was pragmatic, and simply accepted the realities of her condition in a graceful, positive manner. I can't imagine being this well adjusted.

Her friends and I had arranged and planned a surprise party to commemorate her 85 years. And surprised she was, pleasantly so. We had agreed previously that she would spend a couple days with a dear friend of hers, so when the party wound down, I took her to their home. I felt like my child was going off to boarding school.

Muriel's surprise 85th birthday party.

It was the first time in nine months that my mother and I had been apart. And it was one of the first times in almost a year that I gave my undivided attention to the dogs. Xelie had done a magnificent job while I'd been emotionally absent. No one seemed the worse for wear and, true to form, no one held a grudge. I was there right now and that was all that mattered to them. How amazing...

Two days later when I returned for my mother, she announced she wanted to go to Assisted Living. Hell, the ink was barely dry on the sale of her house. And in the span of her micro visit away from home, she and her friend had picked out a place.

If I'm honest, it felt as if she couldn't get away from me fast enough. In retrospect, I think there was a grain of truth in this; and rightfully so. I mean, in the end, I hadn't been the poster child for empathy. I had exerted my will on her in much the same manner as I might have done with a dog in training. My intentions had been good, but I'd forgotten how to listen and respect her desires as an individual.

Thinking back, I suspect that subconsciously I felt my world spiraling out of control, and my knee-jerk was to attempt to control everything, even my own mother.

She expressed, matter-of-factly, that she didn't want to be a burden. That it would be better this way. She was probably right. Had she stayed, I wouldn't have been able to help myself; I would have continued down the path I had been on for months and our relationship might have deteriorated until it died all together. You know the saying "Mother knows best". In this case it was so...

Xelie not happy.

16.

Back on the hamster wheel

By now, after almost eleven months of part time work, I was walking a financial tight rope. To say I was living on the edge would not be quite accurate; I was clawing my fingernails into the precipice, barely able to hang on.

Before the last stick of my mother's furniture had been moved, I had booked my schedule full time, planned trips to my out of town facilities, and entered a couple dog trials.

One problem, my official ranch caretaker was now retired and resided in Assisted Living. My pet sitter agreed to step into the vacant position. No one, not even Mother Theresa, could have filled my mother's shoes in this department.

Upon returning home from my first Houston gig in more than a year, Xelie informed me that we were going to need a different arrangement. She was not happy. This was the first time in all my trips away, over all the years, that she was visibly unsettled upon my return.

My pet sitter was overworked and, in her defense, explosive diarrhea had spread through the kennel while I was away. She was not happy, and after looking at Xelie, neither was I.

I needed the Houston trips; they were essential. I made more money in one week there than I made in three at my home facility. I came up with a plan...

I retrofitted my small travel trailer, transforming the front area into space enough for eight crates. Problem, I had fifteen dogs by this time -- three retired, nine competitors, and three in training.

The marathon working trips would be too hard on the elder retirees, Xelie and Nell. At thirteen, they needed to be pampered and loved as my mother had always done. I found the answer to my prayers; a dear friend, who loved animals, was willing to take Xelie, Nell and one other into her own home while I was away. I insisted on paying for her kindness.

And when I returned from my next week-long trip away, Xelie was happy, excitedly leaping up and down again as she had always done in the past. This arrangement, as labor intensive as it was on my part, was going to work.

So back on the hamster wheel I went, returning to sixty-plus hour work-weeks; returning to my previous arrangement with my canine co-workers and staff. I guess if you look for the positive, at least I was more present for my pack than I had been in the year prior when I'd been caring for my mother.

For the next six months, I kept up the manic pace, desperately trying to replenish my depleted bank account.

I was, again, in pursuit of the points necessary to qualify for the National Finals. A number of local trials had been cancelled, leaving me unsure whether or not Molly, now eleven years old, would have a sufficient amount to qualify. In all likelihood, at her advanced age, this would be her last year in competition.

There was a five-day competition in Colorado, perhaps there I could pick up the points Molly needed. But how? The financial equation of entries, gas and time away from work, didn't quite add up to the amount I'd allotted for a few local trials.

Did I mention that by now, after eight years in Texas, I had some of the most incredible friends I have ever known in my entire life? The film business had left me cynical about humans and their greed and self-centered agendas, but the group of friends that surrounded me now were generous, genuine and caring.

One of these friends, Angie, invited me to ride with her and share expenses. I was accustomed to being in control of my travel and all aspects connected therewith. I could come and go as I pleased, do as I please, without the consideration of another individual. I was used to my independence. And as I'm sure you've gathered, I was a control freak. Just how badly did I want to go to Colorado? This is absolutely no reflection on her...

I left a few days early to practice in a larger space. Then before I knew it, we were on the road. My travel partner and friend was more than generous, supplying crates enough to accommodate my ten dogs in her toy hauler dog room. For the first time in ten years I was traveling in someone else's rig.

Xelie, Nell and two others went to camp, commencing an almost two-week stay with their beloved Aunt Sue, my friend who cared for them in her home.

As Angie and I embarked on the journey, I was somewhat apprehensive hoping that when we returned home our friendship would still be intact.

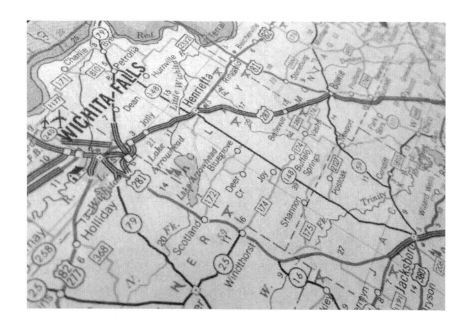

17.

The lights are on but no one's home

I was looking forward to the trial; I had wanted to go for years but had never had the financial wherewithal to make that desire a reality. We had allotted two days for the trip. We were a little over four hours on the road and so far so good, my control freak nature was completely under control and we were actually having an enjoyable time. Google maps declared it a fourteen-hour trip, which only left ten hours to go. Piece of cake...

As we passed through Wichita Falls, we laughed, carelessly making disparaging remarks about the worth of such a place and the character of those who would choose to live there.

A short distance later, a car pulled up beside us, delivering the Universe's reply to our thoughtless comments. They signaled we should pull over. And when we did, we discovered that the sound we'd thought was gravel extricating itself from the tire treads upon leaving the last gas station, had actually been a blow out. Thank God we'd been going so slowly when it happened.

Standing on the side of the freeway, we surveyed the damage. The back right trailer tire was nothing but stringy scraps of rubber, and bits of mangled plastic dangled from the damaged wheel well, bearing witness to the explosive event. Clearly we needed a new tire, at the very least.

Thank god for the iPhone and the iPad as I can't imagine how long it would have taken otherwise to resolve our problem. And no sooner had we found someone to come replace the tire, than we were accosted by a distinct, unsettling odor – gasoline.

Upon closer inspection we discovered the volatile substance dripping from the trailer undercarriage, just behind the damaged wheel well and directly under the toy hauler room where all of my beloved dogs were housed. This was not good.

It took more than an hour for the tire to arrive, and another half hour to change it. Our rescuers examined the gas leak but were at a loss; tires were their specialty, not ginormous fifth wheel trailers. They suggested the mechanic back at their shop could look it over.

We'd already been on the internet and phone attempting to find a trailer repair facility that could accommodate her make and model and that could take us right away. We weren't having much luck. We decided to follow the tire men to their garage.

As we started down the road, Angie commented that, in the event we were unsuccessful with the repair, we needed to consider turning back and going home. Not what I wanted to hear. I needed those points on Molly and I'd already spent a small fortune on entry fees, a fortune that would not be refunded at this late date.

You might have gathered up to now that perseverance in the face of adversity was more than a minor theme in my life. While we made our way to the garage and while the mechanic looked over the damage, I ran scenarios. For years in the movie business I'd been a Production Manager and Line Producer, the job was to schedule and solve problems, both expected and unexpected. I was a professional at running scenarios.

Two hours later, I'd found a repair facility. We'd have to back track to our precious Wichita Falls, but they'd agreed to look at it. Whether or not they could administer repairs depended on what time we arrived.

So back we went to the city we'd dissed. If we weren't careful, we'd be spending more time in Wichita Falls than any other town on this trip. The scenario of returning all the way home was still on the table and rightfully so, as much as I didn't want to acknowledge it.

Thanks to a GPS malfunction that had taken us to nowhere on a remote country road, we arrived at the RV Repair just ten minutes before closing. It was now almost 100 degrees outside and, with the gas leak, we didn't want to run the onboard generator for fear of a tragic mishap. Without the generator, we couldn't run the air conditioning in the dog room. What a relaxing trip this was turning out to be…

I have never met nicer people than those repairmen in Wichita Falls. And after all of our uncharitable remarks… As I took my dogs out of the sweltering trailer one by one, tying them out in the shade, those three men stayed past closing time to repair the RV.

They were light hearted, funny and, in the end, quite competent. Perhaps it was the fact that I had playfully promised that if they could get us on the road that evening, my younger more attractive friend would bestow favors the likes of which they could only imagine in their wildest dreams. Or perhaps they felt sorry for us, knowing our trip may be aborted if we were delayed too long. Whatever the case, by six thirty that evening, they had us back on the road.

Angie and I agreed, no more snide remarks. We drove until just before sunset and, quite by chance, saw a Travel Trailer signaling to turn just ahead. It was an RV park, and quite a nice one as it turned out, with a great place to let the dogs stretch their legs.

We were still in Texas, in the middle of nowhere, as we closed our eyes on the first day of our trip. I texted Aunty Sue to check on Xelie and the gang, as I always did when I was away. I fell asleep that night knowing they were just fine.

photo by Bob Degus

18.

To put things in perspective

We got on the road early the next morning. It wasn't more than a few hours until we crossed the Colorado border. And as we did, I phoned a friend victoriously declaring we were finally out of Texas. I joked, with our luck, the four hour drive to the trial site would probably only take 24 more hours. Ha, very funny!

Not. No sooner had I hung up the phone, than we saw brake lights up ahead on the small highway. The cars were stopping. And then so did we. Unbelievable! Were we ever going to get there?

I was beginning to get annoyed; I had never had so many delays on a road trip, ever; first the tire, and then the gas leak and now this? And what was this, why were we stopped? Didn't they know we had a dog trial to attend?

We sat there for an eternity. We saw smoke in the distance. Time passed, more slowly than usual. Impatient, I got out of the truck to explore what was causing our delay. I wasn't the only curious one. By now, people were out of their cars, chatting on the side of the road.

I intercepted a gentleman who was headed back, having solved the mystery. It was an accident, he explained, and a very bad one at that. About that time, a few vehicles started to trickle toward us in the oncoming lanes.

I hurried back to the truck. But still we waited. It was another half hour before traffic started to move in our lanes. And as we cruised slowly down the road, now two hours behind schedule, we caught our first glimpse of the hold-up.

A car smoldered, totaled and overturned on the shoulder of the road. As we rolled slowly past the crumpled hull, I couldn't imagine a scenario for survival. Two hours earlier, who ever had been in that car, driving to whatever destination they had in mind, with whatever plans they had for the day, or the week, or the years to come; that person, or persons, had just had their world, and all those things they felt were important, permanently interrupted at the moment of impact.

It was a sobering experience. At the same instant I had been annoyed at a small delay, because I had to get to my god almighty important dog trial, this individual, or individuals, had been fighting a losing battle for their lives.

Lets just say it put things in perspective. We drove in silence for quite some time after that. The universe was speaking to me loud and clear. Now if only I could hear.

photo by Bob Degus

19.

Finally...

We pulled into Colorado Springs astounded to see what looked like snow on ground. It was late May. As it turned out, it was hail, piles of it; a freak storm had rolled through as we'd made our final approach into town.

The dirt road up the hillside to the trial field was now impassable. It would be at least two hours before we could make the drive in. This was the longest "fourteen hour" trip I had ever made.

It was just before sunset when we finally parked. The trial field was beautiful, all that I had hoped for. Traversing the foothills complete with nooks, crannies, hilltops and gullies, it was challenging to be sure. But that was the fun of it.

Earlier in the day, I had gotten myself worked up over Molly's number of qualifying points, or lack thereof. I could feel the dark-side of my competitive nature lurking in the shadows of my mind. I really wanted those extra points.

Thankfully, Angie was courageous enough to be quite frank and direct. She reminded me that not long ago at a trial that shall remain unnamed, I had donned this same mind set and my dogs had performed less than spectacularly.

It was at that very trial that she had suggested I remember why I had gotten into working dogs in the first place. It was because I loved dogs, and I marveled at the incredible work they could do on livestock. I had gotten into this for the love of the dogs and the love of the working partnership. Not for competition or for winning – or in this case, for the points.

I thank God for her reminder, and for her actually. I needed to keep things in perspective; what was really important? As if that car accident hadn't shoved it right in my face. This would only be the beginning of a horrifying realization that would later become a little more clear; I'd lost sight of what was important, long, long ago, and I was going to need a set of glasses much stronger than the ones I wore, if I dreamed of seeing in the future.

For the next four days I ran my dogs in the trial. With my new "old" mind set, I enjoyed them and the work beyond all imagination. They were running fabulously, on sheep and a field, the challenges of which some had never seen. I was so very proud and delighted with all of them.

Despite placing in the top ten percent with many of my runs, a theme was beginning to emerge. There were countless times my dogs and I laid down a winning run and timed out as sheep were walking in the pen. It had happened to Molly almost every run. I had been mistakenly disqualified by the judge's own admission, on a run tied for first place. This was not going to be a competition where I emerged victorious, in first place with prize money.

If I was here to stroke the dark side of my competitive nature, I was going to be sadly disappointed. But somehow, this was almost okay. Sure I could have used the money, but I didn't want to go there. My dogs were smiling at me again and that was reward enough.

Until the last day. It was the double-lift; extremely difficult. Two outruns, over terrain, a long course at high altitude. Molly was eleven. This would be a challenge for a young dog. In spite of my improved attitude, as we headed to the post, the challenge awaiting, I was painfully aware Molly was still in need of points.

She went out beautifully, lifted smoothly, and fetched the dogleg on-line, dropping the sheep precisely on the designated spot. She looked back flawlessly, then took off for the second group. But when she arrived, there were no sheep; set-out had allowed them to drift fifty plus yards down into a ravine out of sight.

Now, a dog at her level, with her experience, should be able to listen to direction and find her way to the sheep whether she could see them or not. Molly stopped, waiting for my whistle. But before I could blow, a freak fifty mile-an-hour wind began to blast right in my face. Molly couldn't hear a thing.

As we pulled out of our campsite and headed home, tears trickled down my cheeks. It was, most probably, one of the very last times I would run Molly on a world-class course such as this. She had been magnificent. Why did the universe want us to fail? The question rolled over and over in my mind.

Molly was on the floor by my feet. To her the world was all-good. In fact, it was better than usual; she was riding in the truck beside me. She was in the present. I was a pathetic time traveler, surfing perilously back and forth between past and future. Every year Molly had trialed, she had qualified for the Finals. I sat there, devastated by the fact that she might not have enough points to qualify for the last National Finals of her career.

One might think, with all that had happened in my life over the years and in the microcosm of this trip, that I might have begun to accept the reality that I wasn't fully in charge of my destiny. I'd made the National Dean's list in college for chrissakes; I thought I was smart...

Finally, as Colorado Springs grew smaller and smaller in the rearview mirror, the tears dried and the heavy heart lifted. The remainder of the trip was delightfully uneventful; in fact it was actually quite fun.

The following day, late in the afternoon, amidst a beautiful spring shower, we arrived back at Angie's house safe and sound. It had been raining for days and the roads were flooded. I hadn't slept well in weeks and I was exhausted. As much as I wanted to return home to see Xelie and Nell, I decided the safer more prudent thing to do was get a good night's sleep and return the next day.

photo by Bob Degus

20.

And I thought the past thirteen years were bad...

Well, I wouldn't call it a good night's sleep but at least I'd closed my eyes for a few hours. Still exhausted, I got up the following morning and headed home, pulling my travel trailer loaded with dogs behind me.

I was greeted at my front gate by a small pup, a Jack Russell mix, very cute and very friendly. Aunty Sue was in the barnyard, having just arrived to drop off Xelie, Nell and the others. I handed the pup off to her so I could pull my truck and trailer inside the gate.

We visited briefly before I let Xelie and Nell out to visit. They were happy to see me, and I them. The pack was now reunited and everyone was very curious about the small interloper.

The puppy wore no collar, but I suspected it belonged with two other dogs I'd seen running down the road toward a dead end, when I'd arrived home.

Ever helpful, Sue said she'd take the pup and see if she could find where the other two dogs lived. And that she did. A short time later, she stopped back at my gate to tell me the little rascal was home safe and sound at the end of the road.

A happy ending for all. Sue had only been gone a minute or two when the little pup returned. This would be the theme for the day as I made a number of attempts to return the dog to its rightful owners.

I saw the other two dogs when I approached the house for the first time. There was no one home and there was no way the fence was going to hold this little fella. Of course he followed me back.

I had a long "to do" list and errands to run. I didn't want the pup to get hurt or run over, so I put him in one of my kennel runs for safekeeping. I went to the neighborhood contact list and called and emailed a message to the owners that I had their missing pup. Hopefully they would be home when I returned.

After several hours I was back. No reply message or email. Back down the road I went with the puppy. There was now a truck in the drive. Someone was home. I knocked, several times, no one answered. I put the puppy and his two friends on the front porch then closed and barricaded the gate. They were all still confined when I drove away.

I only had one errand left on my list. My travel trailer needed to be dumped. So out the drive I went, trailer in tow. The RV park was close by and in no time I was headed home, grateful to see my workday finally drawing to a close.

I turned down that beautiful tree lined country road leading to home when a school bus rolled over the hill a short distance away, headed in my direction. As I mentioned early on, this quaint little street was extremely narrow. It was barely big enough for two compact cars to pass, much less my dually, trailer and a school bus.

The bus did not slow down. I didn't want to back out, blind, onto the main road, so I started to pull as close to my side of the road as possible. The bus was on top of me now. There was no room. She kept coming, I kept inching over into the brush when…

"Hey lady! You're wrecking your trailer!" I got my first look at the bus driver, a red-neck poster girl. And at that very moment, my truck could no longer move. I was stuck on something.

The bus still hadn't stopped; this insane keeper and chauffeur to our youth was inching past my rig with less than two inches clearance.

I got out of my truck and was horrified to see my happy little travel trailer impaled on an overhanging tree. I had a serious bout of Tourette's, a silent one; after all, there were children present. But not for long. The bus driver finally cleared my trailer and was on her way, without so much as thinking about placing her foot on the brake.

It took what seemed like an eternity to get unstuck. I didn't want to wreck my truck too. Finally, I was free. I got out and surveyed the damage. It was bad; the top was crunched like an aluminum can with holes punctured in the side and roof.

It was supposed to rain. Yippee, are we having fun yet? All I needed was to get rain damage on top of everything else.

It was 4:40 when I phoned my local RV repair; they closed at 5pm. They were twenty minutes away. Thankfully, they agreed to wait. I pulled in a driveway to turn around. After ten minutes of jimmying the trailer back and forth on the narrow road, I was on my way.

Was nothing stress free in my life? I now had ten minutes; I called back and begged the RV serviceman to wait. Thankfully he agreed. I was sooo tired; I just wanted to be home and finished.

Over an hour later, having dropped the trailer off, I arrived back at my front gate. Well, at least I don't have to worry about the puppy. No sooner had I stepped out of my truck to unlock the gate, than that persistent pup bounded out of the tall grass. Ugh... I wasn't done for the day after all.

Back down the road I went, puppy in tow. I climbed my neighbor's steps once again and knocked. Much to my relief, the door swung open. He was two hundred and fifty plus, no shirt, no zipper in his tattered shorts and a rope for a belt. He did however have all his teeth, at least in the front...

Damaged travel trailer.

I handed over the puppy as he explained how he had lost his phone. Wanting to know how far his canine toddler had traveled, he inquired where I lived. God help me, I told him. Somehow, I graciously disengaged from the conversation and started for home, locking the gate behind me.

That evening I sat outside with my frolicking pack, completely cut-off from any true interaction. I was exhausted and imprisoned by my thoughts and fears for the future. The trailer damage was extensive; it could very well be totaled.

Not a huge deal to someone with financial resources perhaps, but to me... That trailer represented freedom; freedom to go to dog trials, freedom to travel to other facilities where I could earn the extra income that allowed me to stay in business.

Without a trailer I was going nowhere. Sadly I didn't realize I was going nowhere even with a trailer.

This was just the tip of the iceberg. It felt like the Titanic was sinking and I didn't have a life vest. There were sooo many things that needed repair – my house foundation had shifted, the windows needed replacing, the back porch support beams were cracking, and everything needed paint. The dead trees needed burning, the back corner needed clearing, the kennel needed a skirt of cement to shore up the eroding sand. The list went on and on, a list that could easily consume 50K before you reached the end. And then, of course, if you were really seeking a stress rush, there was the mortgage and credit card debt I carried.

I had seven thousand dollars, for everything. Now I wasn't a math major, but clearly I was a bit short.

I had been strong for a very long time. For the past thirteen years many of the challenges had been quite intense, and for the past thirteen years, all of Xelie's life, I'd fought back, I'd persisted.

But that night, sitting in my chair, I was overwhelmed. I needed more than a GPS to find my way out of this one.

21.

What can I do?

The next day, true to form, I attempted to pull myself up by my boot-straps. I had to do something; it was just my nature. And I believe had I not, I would have hit rock bottom, right then and there. Little did I know, that fun awaited me in the not-to-distant future.

I had worked all morning and was in for lunch, contemplating scenarios and checking my e-mail, when the dogs, in both my kennel and in my house, all began to bark. It was my live-in-the-country alarm system; they always let me know someone was here.

I headed to the back door. Outside, my newly acquainted lost pup neighbor was lurking. Not the kind of company I wanted or expected. He hadn't knocked; he was just looking around.

"Can I help you?" I asked, not particularly friendly. His puppy was lost again. Shocking. I hadn't seen him since the day I returned him, and told him so. I was happy to see the man go, and would be happy to never see him again.

I stepped back in the house and gazed at the seven dogs crated in my dining room, and more were coming in for training in the next couple weeks. As much as I enjoyed seeing them and visiting with them when I'd come in and out during a normal work day, the fact was, having them all live inside was creating a terrible mess. The amount of dirt and sand they'd track in with the morning dew would have kept an army of maids working full time.

The puppies had already damaged the wall. I stood there, feeling as if everything was in decay. Maybe if I could just clean up the inside of the house; maybe that would help.

It was almost June, and inevitable that the infernal summer heat was on its way. I had a room in my carport kennel that would accommodate more than a dozen dogs quite nicely, but there was no air conditioning, they'd certainly overheat.

Years earlier, when I had first moved in, I had a bid done to cool that room. I'd been quoted $3000. On that day in late May, I resolved that if I could get it done for under a thousand dollars, that's what I'd do.

Thankfully, I was able to make that equation materialize. On my next day off, I'd begin the project.

Before I could move the dogs the room needed to be cleaned, really cleaned. You see, I'd used it as a storage and feed room for the past eight years, and beneath the fresh alfalfa there was eight years of dust, mold and old hay.

And then there was the small problem of where to put the feed? I had an empty stall in the barn with a gate I could lock, only problem was that the stall enclosure could be easily penetrated by the sheep.

I think the sheer panic of my situation, gave me the strength to move those heavy panels all by myself. At a good one hundred plus pounds each, they'd been donated a number of years prior, but had always been so unwieldy and heavy, I'd never used them – not until now.

Somehow I got them in the stall, and a few hours later, the new feed room was built and loaded with food. On to the deep cleaning of the carport room...

That took hours of sorting and tossing unused items stored there. Followed by more hours of shoveling and sweeping and breathing god knows what. Finally it was finished. Sue's friend ran the electric and installed the new AC unit. As the sun set that day, the room began to cool, awaiting the dogs that would soon call it home.

It was the middle of the night when I began to feel ill. By four in the morning, I knew there was no way I could give lessons that day. Thank God for my i-Phone; I could cancel all my appointments without leaving my bed.

For the next two days I lay there, nauseous, achy and weak. And I slept. And slept. And slept. I slept for almost forty-eight hours straight. Again my dear friend Sue came to the rescue.

She'd let my bedroom dogs out, then returned with supplies to do battle with the bug. I couldn't drink the anti-nausea medicine quickly enough. "You might want to keep an eye on Xelie", she'd said and explained that she seemed to be urinating quite a bit.

When I inquired if Xelie was out with the sheep, Sue quickly left the room. Long story short, there were no injuries, but Xelie had seized the opportunity to indulge in her passion for sheep. Thank God everyone survived, I thought.

Amidst the fog of this mystery illness, as I went to cancel yet more appointments, I received a disturbing and rather frightening e-mail. It was from Mr. Lost Puppy. All in caps, he called me a liar and accused me of taking his pup and turning it over to the pound. And now, a week later, when he'd finally thought it prudent to contact the shelter to see if they had him, he'd been informed that his precious pup had already been adopted by someone else.

His daughter's life and his own were ruined. And, you got it – IT WAS ALL MY FAULT. He ended the angry email tirade with words that disturbed me more than any of the others. "WHAT GOES AROUND, COMES AROUND".

What did he mean? I crawled out of bed, and hunched over in the clenches of nausea, I shuffled slowly out to my kennel. There was no way my dogs were sleeping outside where I couldn't look after them, not after receiving that psychotic email.

I went on the record with the police department without filing a report, just in case... And asked that they send a car to patrol whenever they could.

Then headed back to get some more flu-induced sleep. I believe I was allotted a six-inch sliver of bed-space that evening as I slept with eight dogs in my room.

Finally, on Saturday, I was able to resume lessons. I was a bit weak and decided to use my ATV to help me make it through the day. It was still morning when it sputtered and died just outside my small training pen. I'd just had it fixed less than a month before. One more thing to add to my list...

Let's see, since I returned home, I'd totaled my trailer, gotten deathly ill, been threatened by a psycho, broken my ATV, to mention only a few. Almost everyday, there had been something. God knows, we wouldn't want things to be too easy.

photo by Bob Degus

22.

The beginning…

I should have known better than to utter the words "What else could go wrong?" That evening Xelie was keeping me company in the kitchen. I'd been so absent of late, emotionally and literally, and there she stood, that incredible face staring back at me.

I bent over and gave her a big hug. And as I did, my hand slid over something under her front right shoulder, in the armpit area. A bump, distinct, new. I didn't like the feel of it. We were well into the evening by now and she looked completely fine. She smiled back at me as if to say "What?"

I decided to take her to my vet first thing on Monday morning. I went to bed that evening worried, hoping it was just some fatty cyst like the one she had a little further down on her ribcage.

Somewhere in the middle of Saturday night before the dawn of Sunday morning, I decided to give Xelie a thorough going over. And when I did, I found more – some on her neck and one under her right hip. Not good.

It wasn't yet 10 a.m. on Monday. My vet ran her hands over that beautiful scruffy wheaten body. The exam didn't take long. "Lymphoma. It looks like lymphoma…"

The world stood still.

"I'm sorry", she said. Which meant only one thing…

My mind was whirling as she showed me even more lumps than I'd already discovered. Nodes I didn't even realize existed were swollen.

How could I not know? I'd been so caught up in all my troubles, maybe if I'd taken the time to actually pay attention… I felt like an awful, terrible, neglectful parent. My only consolation was that Sue hadn't noticed either and she was as far from neglectful as she could be. The truth was, I had been less than ideal, but in my defense the lumps were also tucked away in places that I never would have thought to pet.

Before I left the office, my vet had set up an appointment with a specialist for the very next day. There was no cure, but treatments had improved, she informed me. I had never believed in chemotherapy for animals, especially if there was no chance for recovery. On the other hand, I never had advanced notice that one of my beloved dogs was living with a defined end not far in sight. I would talk to the specialist…

Shell shocked, I drove home, glancing in the rearview at Xelie sitting happily in the back seat. Surprising… She'd never been a big fan of car rides. In fact, she is the only dog I have ever known that, given a choice, would sit backward in the front passenger seat, facing the seat. Always. It wasn't the most stable of positions and, as a result, I think it made the ride uncomfortable.

I had always fancied that this position harkened back to her puppyhood. When she was young and we'd go see sheep, my husband would drive and Xelie would ride with me in the passenger seat, in my lap, facing me. I always thought it odd.

As she grew older, maybe riding that way reminded her of happier times and of something she loved. Maybe she thought if she rode that way she'd get sheep. Maybe she was trying to tell me something; like retirement was really not what she had in mind. This is all in retrospect you understand....

Anyway, we were in my mother's Honda and there wasn't enough room for her in the front seat so she sat in the back that day. And stretched out like any other normal dog would be, she was happy to ride.

Tears, those damn tears... I didn't want her to see.

It was one of those cliché moments that seemed anything but that to me. I had taken her for granted for so very long. And now we were looking at two to four more weeks with no treatment.

I had lost only four dogs in my life, each passing had been devastating and the grief had been almost unbearable. Three of them had been sudden, and Annie had only been four days. Two to four weeks...

I just kept looking at her; you wouldn't have known a thing was wrong. Over the last year, she'd been a tiny bit less active and had been sleeping a bit more soundly, but she was thirteen years old, ninety-one in dog years. And she was a large breed, which meant her dog-year equivalent was probably well over one hundred.

"I need less dogs". I'd said it over and over in the past six months as things had been building to a crisis point. My 2013 tax return was the wake-up call – line item total for veterinary expenses on the dogs had exceeded 11k. The writing was on the wall.

But not like this, not Xelie. Be careful what you wish for... And how you send that message into the universe. I should have been more specific. "I want to place some of my dogs, or sell some of my dogs", to a hand-picked homes, of course. Xelie dying of lymphoma? This was not the scenario I was talking about.

And there she was, fit as many dogs half her age. We parked in the usual spot just inside my front gate. I opened the back door and out she came, leash already attached. You see the sheep were out and I didn't want any trouble. She glanced over at them now and again as we made our way to the house. And the thought, the tearful thought, how may more times would we be able to do this simple thing, walk together toward the house?

I looked at all my dogs a little differently that evening, as they wrestled and chased under Xelie's watchful eye. But mostly I watched Xelie. Now that I knew, what next?

photo by Bob Degus

23.

The calm before the storm

Storm clouds loomed on the horizon, bigger than usual and black, very black. As I started into the house to check on the weather, I caught sight of Cora. She had looked slightly different to me in the last number of days; I didn't remember her jaw muscles being quite so pronounced, and the muscles between her ears, were they bigger?

I hated my progressive lenses. I can't tell you how many times I'd glance down at my legs and think, my God you've gotten fat. And then taken them off to realize I looked just as I always had. Maybe it's the same with Cora. I took off my glasses and looked – hmmm… Probably just a

photo by Bob Degus

little over vigilant now, after Xelie.

I went in the house and looked at the weather forecast; it was bad, very bad, with tornado warnings and all. Wouldn't it be ironic if a cyclone whisked us away tonight, now that I was planning on two to four more weeks with Xelie? How many times would the universe need to remind me that I didn't really know what I thought I knew, and that having control of my future was simply a grand illusion?

A cool wind kicked up dust and heralded the storm's soon arrival. I had just put the last dog up and headed toward the house with Xelie, Nell and the other members of the house-dog cast.

We only lasted a short time up in my second-story bedroom, when the storm became too intense to remain. Xelie didn't like thunderstorms and she was really quite upset; she was not the only one.

I grabbed the bottle of dog appeasing pheromone and quickly sprayed Xelie's collar, and then the others. We headed into the living room where I sat on the couch waiting for it to take effect. I kept Xelie close,

photo by Bob Degus

stroking her, rubbing her ears, trying to instill calm through my touch. She was already terminal, she didn't need to be scared to boot.

Xelie had always been a courageous dog, ready to take on a challenge, prepared to defend any member of her beloved pack if necessary. Her stormaphobia always seemed out of character. But there you have it, even the strongest most independent of characters still have their vulnerabilities. I was happy I could be there to comfort her.

What does she have to live for? The question rolled over and over in my mind. She spends much of her day sleeping in my room or looking out the window barking at the sheep action in the field. Sure she gets out in the morning and evening, and yes, she does have her best friend Nell, and she still is the undeniable pack leader. But is this enough? To her, is this quality of life? I gazed at her, mulling over the question when…

My cell phone rang; it was Angie, the woman I'd traveled with to Colorado. She said she was calling to warn me about the storm, but looking back, I think she knew I needed someone to talk to.

Xelie sat with me as I had one of the most philosophical conversations I'd had in years. I almost didn't notice the storm as it hit full force, wind whistling through sheets of torrential rain, lit up as if by a strobe, as lightning cut jagged through the darkness. Hail pattered on the windowpanes, punctuated by cracks of thunder. The weathermen had been right; this was a substantial gale.

We discussed the meaning of life, explored what reality was in actuality, and theorized about why we are born into existence on this planet. In the end, the bottom line was we had our ideas but the ultimate truth was simply unknowable. In the past thirteen years I had barely taken time to think of what I might wear that day, much less delve into meaningful topics such as these.

Sitting here now, I realize these topics, knowable or unknowable should never be forgotten or pushed too far out of sight. The universe is a compelling mystery and to those who are looking, it is more than willing to provide poetic hints to help the seeker unravel the tip of its unfathomable nature.

I can tell you without a doubt, that without Xelie, without the realization that I'd been taking her so for granted and that soon, very soon, I'd be forever without her; without all this, that beautiful philosophical conversation would most certainly have not existed.

Without Xelie, I'd still be imprisoned in my workaholic chaos and crisis; oblivious to much of the beauty around me, taking for granted those wonderful things that exist in my world.

Xelie, the morning before going to the specialist.

24.

Time, more or less...

We got up early the next day. It was one of the most stunning mornings I've ever seen. The storm had washed everything clean of dust and the sky was a crisp deep royal blue. Moisture glistened from the grass like tiny diamonds in the morning light. It was cool, and for June, that was a miracle in and of itself.

Xelie and I stepped out the back door; her appointment with the specialist was at nine and we had more than an hour's drive ahead of us. Her big yellow paws left tracks behind as they cut through the wet grass. As I watched her peruse the vast array of delectable scents, it occurred to me I had very few pictures of her. It's never too late, I thought. I pulled my phone from my pocket and hit the camera icon.

I took a dozen pictures as we made our way to the car. My favorite? Xelie, perched atop the sand, lying there regal and tall like ranchette royalty, with sheep as a backdrop, fenced in the barnyard behind her. It's a beautiful photo, I thought as I looked over what I'd shot. And looking at it now, it <u>is</u> a wonderful photograph – of Xelie separated from her sheep.

We made it to the specialist with just a few minutes to spare. It wasn't long before they ushered us into an exam room. Xelie had never been frightened of vets, and today was no exception. Nose in the lead, she explored the room and the invisible residue left behind by others, both canine and feline. She then settled comfortably to the floor, waiting. Or was she waiting? I wondered if she wondered why we'd come here to hang out?

Before long, a friendly technician greeted us, asked a few questions, then escorted Xelie out of the room and into the back for further examination and a biopsy.

It wasn't long before Xelie and the specialist returned to the room with a confirmed diagnosis of lymphoma. She went over the options – no treatment Xelie had 2-4 weeks. With steroid treatment she might have 2-3 months and with chemotherapy, possibly up to six months. But there were no guarantees that anything would change, even with treatment. Like there ever are any guarantees...

She went on to explain what the disease would look like and, thankfully, she said Xelie would never be in a lot of pain. She'd just grow weaker and weaker, and sleep more and more, until the end finally came.

The doctor left Xelie and me alone, in that cold air-conditioned room, to think over our options. Xelie lay comfortably on the hard cement floor. Everyone had commented on what great shape she was in, especially for a dog her age. But great shape or not, her days were numbered. And possibly, depending on our decision, that number could be altered.

As I said before, I never considered chemotherapy a viable option, especially in a case where there was no chance for healing or returning to a healthy life. But there was Xelie, on the floor beside me. I ran my fingers through her wiry hair. The question here was time, and how much or how little?

The clarity I'd always had was becoming clouded by my attachment to her. So many thoughts raced through my mind, but in the end they boiled down to one simple question – who are we buying time for, Xelie or me? I guess there was another option; we could have been buying time for both of us... I left the office that day with my beloved Xelie and a bottle of steroids. I had seven days to decide whether or not we wanted to pursue chemotherapy, after that there was no going back.

If only I could ask Xelie what she wanted. If only she could tell me.

photo by Bob Degus

25.

Talk to me...

I decided on steroid therapy, no chemo. I wanted to keep Xelie as comfortable as possible, and I suspected that chemotherapy would only have made her feel worse, for a longer period. What would be the point in that?

We were already into the beginning of June and experience had shown me the scorching Texas summers were a challenge even for the healthiest of creatures. I asked myself how I would like being sick in the scalding weather to come? The answer came, I wouldn't. So, steroid therapy it was.

As I slid the first prednisone tablet into Xelie, I wondered if she knew she was sick? If she knew she was dying? I wanted more than anything to talk to her. I wanted to know how she wanted to spend the time she had left.

I looked at her, searching... Searching for some answer, even a hint of an answer. If only she spoke English. Even another language would have sufficed; I simply would have gone on the internet, translated and voila! We'd be able to communicate.

But as I gazed at her it was clear, if I wanted to communicate with Xelie, I was going to have to stretch well beyond language. But how? I was very familiar with communicating and reading a dog when I was training them on livestock. But this was different. It wasn't work related. I was an expert at work.

The first thing that occurred to me was to let her have the run of the house. That way I could see her as I went in and out during a work day. I'd never done it in the past for fear someone would accidentally let her out and she'd get into the sheep, in more ways than one. But in light of the situation, it was worth a try. I would simply tell everyone to make sure she didn't slip past them on their way in or out. Why I hadn't thought of it before is beyond me.

She was delighted to have the entire downstairs to reign over. Her eyes twinkled, she felt special for the first time in a very long time.

I sat on the floor beside her; she liked lying on the cool tile and seemed to be happy to have company. I had worked all morning and now it was time for Xelie. True to form, I asked what she'd like to do? She just looked back. It wasn't long before her eyes began to flutter closed; a nap would be nice.

I wanted to spend time with her, but I had client dogs in for training and they needed to be worked. And if she was going to sleep...

As quietly as I could, I started to get up. Xelie's eyes blinked open. She looked at me as if to say, "Where are you going?" I sat back down on the floor, feeling a tinge of guilt about attempting to leave. I stroked the top of her head. Before long, she took a deep breath and closed her eyes once again.

And once again I tried, as stealthily as possible, to get up to go work. But no sooner had I started to rise, than she raised her head and stared at me again.

Why can't I sit and do nothing, even for five minutes? It wasn't just a thought; it was a revelation. I had no idea how to be still. I was so accustomed to having every minute of every day scheduled and filled with work, that to have five minutes unaccounted for seemed unfathomable.

Xelie just gazed at me, without judgment. She didn't speak English, but even so, it was clear she didn't want me to go. I sat back down.

I was a work junkie. At that moment, I knew it without a doubt. I was addicted to work in a way just as destructive as if I'd been addicted to drugs. My addiction was, and had been for quite some time, interfering with my relationship with my dogs. And they were, after all, my best friends.

So difficult as it was, I did not train for the remainder of that day. I attempted to hush the noise in my mind and just "be" with Xelie. And in the quiet of her afternoon nap, a new priority emerged. It was Xelie; she would come first and foremost, even ahead of my all-so-important work.

The fact was, it was financially impossible for me to quit entirely, but I could slow down, I had done it for my mother. And now I'd do it for Xelie. Spoken like a true addict, don't you think?

The following day, my Colorado companion, Angie, came for her weekly lesson. And when we were finished, I discovered she'd left behind a book, "Animal Talk" by Penelope Smith. I sat on the couch, Xelie resting nearby, and began to devour it page by page.

She discussed different avenues of communication with non-human species. But first and foremost, before communication was possible, the human needed to empty their mind to a place of quiet receptiveness. She went on to say animals could speak in symbols, or images or feelings, emotional or physical. That actually speaking English to certain animals sometimes helped...

I studied Xelie... Then asked, "Do you want to go outside?" She leapt to her feet and bounced by the back door. Even a deaf person could hear that her response was a "yes".

Xelie was very excited to be getting outside in the middle of the day. This was unheard of; she must be very, very special. That is what she said as she bounded happily about. I was beginning to pay attention.

It was the first time in God knows how long I simply went on a walk with Xelie, just with her alone. And it was the first time ever that I didn't control the walk, that I didn't mandate where we were going and what we were doing. If I wanted Xelie to communicate with me, I surmised, then I'd have to let go and simply follow and listen. And I thought being still and not working was difficult?

She stretched into a relaxed trot and headed down into the back field. I trailed after, wondering what she had in mind. Before long we had arrived. Xelie stopped in the cool shade of large oak. As I joined her beneath that glorious tree, she looked back, seemingly surprised that I had cared enough to follow. But happily surprised she was...

"What?" I asked. She moved further beneath the tree to some tall lush grass and gleefully plopped down atop it, rubbing and rolling on her back. To her, this is heaven, I thought. I lay down on the grass nearby; she was right, it was an awesome place. I'd passed by it numerous times, but had never thought to stop, much less taken the time to lie down.

The smell of grass, I hadn't experienced it up close for decades. A light breeze rustled the branches stretched out above. Shadows danced over and around us. Xelie rolled to an upright position and looked over.

Why had she brought me here, to this tree? Was it another lesson about being in the moment, enjoying and delighting in the beauty around us? Or was it something else? Would this place mean something down the road? In my mind, I asked her these questions. She didn't answer, or if she did, I couldn't hear.

It wasn't long before she moved out of the shade. As I rose to my feet I could see where she was headed. The sheep were across the pasture.

Xelie heads toward the sheep, for the first time in years.

They lifted their heads and began to group as she started in their direction. This time Xelie was speaking loud and clear.

I took a deep breath and followed quickly after her. It had been years since I had purposefully allowed Xelie to work sheep and the thought of it made me more than a little nervous.

On the other hand, in respect of our new path, I needed to follow and not control. If I truly wanted Xelie to communicate, then I needed to listen. And here was the first real test.

To say I was apprehensive would be an understatement. But Xelie was older now and she had slowed down, worst case I could probably catch her if anything went awry. Besides, it was the whole adult flock, and in the large group they would be heavy and relatively unreactive. In other words it was the best possible scenario, short of my three beginner sheep.

I was pleasantly surprised as Xelie made contact. She moved around the flock to the right, very workmanlike, and brought them neat as could be, straight toward me. If the hunting instinct still lurked within her,.

photo by Bob Degus

I couldn't see it.

The look on her face said it all, this was a dream come true. She was out in the big pasture, working sheep just like so many others she'd watched from the window in the confines of my second-story bedroom. She had barked and barked, year after year, trying to tell me. But her pleas had landed on deaf self-absorbed ears.

Watching her that afternoon, working the sheep, tucking in stragglers, keeping them grouped together, was truly amazing. I had forgotten what it was like to work Xelie, when Xelie was working and not hunting.

She knew what she was doing and she was beautiful to watch. She would have worked for hours that day had I let her, making up for lost time, making up for all those years I had denied her.

And here she was, being so good. Even at thirteen, all she wanted was to work and be in contact with sheep. I had found the number one thing on her bucket list. I was delighted.

And then devastated. What had I done? How could I have missed the fact that I had denied Xelie the single most important thing in her life, next to being alpha of the pack of course.

I didn't want her to overdo, so as she was beginning to tire, I gently took hold of her collar and led her to a pool of water to cool off. With mixed emotions, I watched as she dunked her nose in deep, then played bowed her front half into the water, moments later dropping her backside on the rim where it overhung the small pool.

This was how she always took a dip on a hot day – front half in, back half out. Different from the others, like sitting backward in the front seat of the car, she had never figured out how to bend her body just enough to fit the whole thing in. Or maybe she knew, but preferred her signature position.

Whatever the case, it didn't matter. Xelie beamed, looking back at the sheep. There was no doubt, this had been the best day she'd had in years.

26.

Xelie on the schedule

That evening as I sat outside with my dogs, I informed Xelie that she was officially on my schedule. I promised she would be up first each day, before any of my clients, because that's how important she was, and I didn't want any circumstance bumping her out of her time slot.

I'm not sure she understood, but she was happy nonetheless. It was a beautiful evening and she was surrounded by the pack she loved.

Molly sidled up to my chair, stick clenched tightly between her teeth, inviting me to engage in a game of toss and fetch. As always, Cora was beside her, waiting for Molly to get careless so she could make off with her stick.

Molly and Cora waiting to fetch stick.

I had been looking at Cora for days and days now. And transition lenses or not, I was certain she looked different; her head was getting bigger and so was her neck. Her collar had become so tight that I'd removed it. My vet was scheduled to come out the next day to give my young dog Jambo some shots; she agreed to look at Cora when she came.

It was bright and early the following morning when I invited Xelie to join me. We stepped out the back door; I had already put up the dogs and let out the sheep. "Where are your sheep?" When I asked, she couldn't believe it; I could tell, even without English.

Her head spun to the pasture below where the sheep moseyed about. With pure delight, she trotted toward them. She had arthritis in her left shoulder and left hip. It gave her a distinctive bob as she moved. But arthritis or not, there was no way Xelie was passing up sheep. It was the second day of a dream come true.

I couldn't remember when I'd last gleaned so much pleasure from working a dog. Except for maybe when she and I had herded the day before. I was thoroughly enjoying rekindling my relationship with Xelie.

And was so grateful to have a little time to make up for my mistakes.

She was unlike any of my other dogs, independent yet affectionate, thoughtful and intelligent yet always her own individual, playful, yet serious, and proactive, rarely reactive. She was a force to be reckoned with, and had always been.

A Picard owner once stated that the breed was to be ruled with an iron fist, wearing a velvet glove. After spending thirteen years with Xelie, I had come to believe that perhaps he was right. He was right if it was control you were after. But now our relationship was evolving; more and more I wanted to know her, not control her.

It was a glorious morning of moving sheep all about. Xelie preferred gathering to the right, avoiding any pressure to her arthritic left side. We'd work for a while, then take a water break in the pool. But only long enough for her to catch her breath, then back to the sheep she'd go. I had allotted an hour, and she used every minute of it.

When we were done, we headed back up the hill toward the house. Droplets of water still dripped from Xelie's beard as she smiled, delighted with the way her morning had begun.

I towel dried her before opening the door. She stepped inside where a delectable selection of foods awaited her. It was like a gourmet buffet, and I had prepared it just for Xelie.

27.

Xelie's buffet

Xelie had always been a finicky eater, skipping meals throughout the years had not been at all uncommon. But now, with taking steroids and being sick, eating had become critical.

The day my vet diagnosed her with lymphoma, I had started her on raw meat. She'd been losing interest in her kibble, both with fixin's and without, and I wanted her diet to be as clean and pure as possible. It had been years since I'd fed a raw diet, cost had made it prohibitive, but I'd always been a staunch believer that it was preferable by far.

In the beginning, the novelty of fresh raw red meat was enticement enough. The others were eating kibble and Xelie knew she was getting special treatment. But when it came to food, she had never been a creature of habit. Variety was the spice of life, and a requirement if you wanted Xelie to eat on a daily basis.

That said, it wasn't long before it became necessary to broaden her culinary horizons beyond raw meat. And thus the birth of Xelie's daily buffet. "Now this is more like it", I could see her say.

It had been quite some time since I had made special trips to the market in search of edible prospects that would appeal. It required a connection, it required remembering and imagining what Xelie might enjoy. And it required time, precious time.

I had forgotten how wonderful it was to make a real commitment to pleasing an animal. Don't misunderstand, all the creatures with which I co-habitated were well cared for, plenty of food and water and time to play. A safe environment, warm in the winter and cool in the summer.

But to make a concerted effort, to go out of my way, to surprise one of my animal companions for the sheer pleasure of watching them delight in the receiving... That I hadn't done in more years than I care to mention.

And now, thanks to Xelie, I was remembering the importance of letting someone, human, canine or otherwise, know just how important they are to us in our lives, not just through words, but through actions.

To me, Xelie was remarkable and I wanted her to know, that I knew just how exceptional she was. She was now more than on my schedule. She was on the top of my list. I loved it and so did she!

We were getting to know each other all over again, like two old friends reunited. We were the same as we'd been ten years before, yet we were different.

Xelie had matured and grown but her spirit was still pure. A creature of the light, she possessed a wisdom the likes of which I'd never seen in an animal or human for that matter. And the more we got re-acquainted, the more I realized I'd only been partially aware, but never fully recognized or appreciated, just how deep her wisdom went.

For the very first time in our relationship, I was willing to meet her as an equal, not as the superior human who always knew best. She was fast becoming my very dearest friend. Honest, direct, non-judgmental and forgiving -- that was Xelie. Boy did I have a lot to learn from her...

So on this beautiful Friday morning, the 13th day of June, the second day in half a dozen years or more that she'd gotten to work her sheep, I toweled Xelie off and opened the back door. She trotted inside and headed directly to the buffet. "See you in a little while" I smiled, then headed out to work.

Jambo

28.

Not again...

My morning with Xelie had left me feeling quite uplifted. I headed into the carport dog room on my way to beginning morning lessons. I had only just entered when I heard it, that distinctive, horrible sound, thumping, a-rhythmic, emanating from inside a plastic crate nearby.

I followed the noise; it was Jambo, a yearling female who was showing tremendous promise in the sheepherding arena. Through the metal door, I could see her sleek feminine body thrashing about spasmodically inside; she was in the throes of a seizure. I quickly opened the crate to make contact. Thankfully, the event didn't last long.

This was not the first seizure Jambo had experienced. There had been two prior episodes, clusters of neurological mayhem that had gone on for hours. The first four thousand dollar visit to the vet, complete with MRI, yielded a diagnosis of idiopathic epilepsy. To a layman that label translates simply to mean they have no idea as to the cause.

The neurologist prescribed medication and there were no more seizures, not until five months later – just following a heat cycle. A pattern was emerging; the first cluster had occurred just following a heat cycle as well. Hormones, those dreaded hormones. And I though menopause was bad... At least there was a solution, I could spay her and hopefully the seizures would stop forever.

But there had been so many crises in the past couple weeks, I hadn't yet taken Jambo for the procedure. And now it seemed my theory was shot to hell. Only three weeks had passed, there had been no additional heat cycle and I'd been religious about her medication. A dark pit weighed heavy in my stomach.

The good news was, she snapped back to being herself rather quickly. She bypassed the post-ictal phase, a period following a convulsion where the dog is disturbed, sometimes unsteady, and definitely not themselves.

The last bout of seizures the doctors had doubled her meds for several days; which I did, right there, on the spot. The seizure had been short of duration, and her recovery quick, all good signs. I'd wait for her second pill to kick in and hope for the best.

The uplifted feeling Xelie had left me with only minutes before had given way to agitation and worry. I began lessons knowing I needed to give the medicine time to work.

Two hours later, the seizures persisted. Jambo was now as post-ictal as she could be. It's a desolate helpless feeling, watching an animal you love held hostage to this disorder. They can't hear you, or feel you, or know that you're there to help, not until the massive neurological misfire runs its course. One can only do one's best to keep the afflicted from harming itself.

The neurologist was calling a bolus medication into the pharmacy, but of course there was a wait. Did I have any liquid valium, they asked? I knew getting angry wasn't going to help matters. I wanted to scream, why the hell didn't you supply me with these medications in the first place, just in case there was an event such as this? Hadn't my two trips to their clinic, earning them almost five thousand dollars plus, bought me the right to be armed for future events?

I took a deep breath and answered that I did not have any valium but perhaps my regular vet, who was scheduled to come out that day, might have the precious solution.

Long story short, after speaking with the neurologist, my vet agreed to give me the valium she had on hand. But now, after the morning's events, there was no way she was giving Jambo her vaccinations, not in this condition. I was in total agreement, although disappointed that she wasn't going to get a look at Cora that day.

We rescheduled our appointment for early the next week and agreed to meet in the pharmacy parking lot when I went to pick up Jambo's bolus meds.

Xelie had insisted on making the drive into town with me. And I wanted her to go. Truth was I wanted her to go everywhere with me. She

leaped happily into the car and we started on our way into town.

I watched her from the rearview, she was staring out the window. I hit the button and the glass began to slide down, allowing a bouquet of fragrances to cascade into the car and wash over Xelie.

Intrigued, she immediately stood up and poked her head out the window. Wind whipped through her beard and tussled the tufts on the end of her ears, as she inhaled the vast array of scents carried by the wind. This was a gourmet buffet of a different kind, that could satiate even the most discerning proboscis.

I smiled. Somehow Xelie could lighten even the darkest of situations. Riding in the car was fast becoming her second most favorite thing to do, next to sheep herding of course.

Our trip into town had been a success and we returned home with valium and bolus in hand. Within an hour, Jambo's seizures had stopped. Jambo didn't join the pack that evening for free time. The drugs were powerful and she needed to recover.

Xelie's sandy throne.

I sat down in the shade and watched Xelie; it was her daily ritual. In the very same spot, not far from my chair, she'd dig into the sand, fluffing it up for maximum comfort and cool. She'd then spin several times before dropping atop it. I called it her Sandy Throne. And from there each evening, she'd reign over her kingdom and her pack of subjects.

It had been a long stressful day. I tried to follow Xelie's example and be in the present, leaving the residual worry behind. I was painfully unsuccessful that evening.

It was difficult enough facing Xelie's diagnosis and, so far, I thought I'd done fairly well riding this horrible wave. But why Jambo, why now? Wasn't the looming loss of my precious heart dog enough? What was the universe trying to tell me and why, why would no one speak plainly and clearly in English?!

29.

John Deere speaks

In the midst of the chaos that week, my insurance company had agreed to fix my travel trailer rather than write it off as a total loss. It was a tremendous relief, as I couldn't afford the payments a newer trailer would have implied. And what I could have purchased with the insurance money would have been more than cause for clinical depression.

I had brought the trailer home, emptied it out and taken it back for repair. What a relief, I'd been granted my freedom after all. It was one thing I could check off my list of needed repairs. The universe had thrown me a bone, so to speak, and I was as grateful as a starving dog might have been to scarf it up.

The weekend was busy, yet uneventful. By Sunday, Jambo was much more herself and I had scheduled a short day to spend quality time with Xelie.

I can't be sure, but I believe we'd gone together to get the mail. In any event, we were making our way back down the driveway toward the house when Xelie veered off into the sand, on a decisive path headed toward what, I didn't know.

It wasn't long before she reached her destination. She stopped beside a John Deere Gator. It belonged to our friend Auntie Sue. Rigged atop the back of the vehicle was a tank with a sprayer.

Sand burrs had become a nuisance in my working field, and dog after dog would limp through them as they trained and moved sheep. Sue wanted to annihilate the prickly offenders once and for all by spraying an herbicidal burr killer with her John Deere rig.

Xelie sniffed the gator then dropped her nose to the ground beside it, just below the sprayer. She looked at me. No more spraying? Is that what you're saying?

I had always hated using chemicals of any kind on the pasture, but had succumbed several times when our goat weed had gotten out of control and made it impossible for dogs to work and train. The sales people had always said that once the chemical dried there were no ill effects to any animals that walked or grazed there. It was like turning a blind eye to a nuclear reactor in your backyard. But here in Texas, chemicals were a way of life. Everyone did it, and so had I.

I promised Xelie no more spraying. What I thought, but didn't say was "while you're still alive". I'm not proud of this, believe me; I felt like a liar. But there were so many things that needed to be done or repaired or fixed – I just didn't have the energy to pick twenty acres worth of weeds on top of everything else.

As we moved back toward the house, I began to wonder if the chemicals had been responsible for Xelie's lymphoma. I'd only sprayed a couple times in the past nine years…

Maybe she was referring to all the chemicals in general. There was the heartworm preventative, the flea and tick applications, and the wide variety of wormers for internal parasites.

Living in California, in what was essentially a desert, none of these chemicals had been a necessity. It was too dry for heartworm carrying mosquitoes or parasites of any kind. Sure there was the occasional tick, but that was rare and usually due to a hike in the mountain forests.

In the hot, humid environs of Texas, these parasitic monsters thrived. And they were no joke. They could kill your dog in any number of horrific manners. I hated using preventative chemicals, but the alternative was much worse. While I lived in Texas, I'd have no choice but to continue.

It wasn't until a day or two later that it occurred to me that she may have been trying to communicate something else or something more. She hadn't see Sue in a few weeks; maybe she was trying to tell me she wanted to see Sue before it was too late. The gator was the only item of Sue's present on the property so it would be the obvious choice if one didn't have language.

Perhaps it was both, she wanted to see Sue and warn me about the chemicals. Perhaps it was neither. Perhaps it was just a coincidence that she'd stopped at the John Deere. You can believe whatever conclusion fits in your comfort zone.

As for me, I believe she was clearly communicating both thoughts. Going to the Gator was "I want to see Sue", and sniffing the ground below the sprayer was her warning about the chemicals. Why not kill two birds, so to speak, with one stop?

Cora's head swells.

30.

And then there were three...

It was now eight days after my vet had diagnosed Xelie with lymphoma. Jambo had been seizure free for more than fifty-two hours. My vet had just finished giving her the last vaccination when I brought Cora downstairs for a looksee.

"You're not crazy", she said as she studied Cora. She confirmed my suspicion that Cora's head, neck and, by now, the rest of her body, had grown larger. And her eyes were indeed bulging, even without transition lenses.

Cora had been on raw meat since the Colorado trip where she so effectively communicated that she was done with kibble and would kill for raw flesh. So as to retain possession of my arm, from a distance I tossed

124

her a small turkey neck at the request of my vet. She wanted to see just how ravenous Cora had become.

Cora voraciously gobbled the fowl neck, her eyes bulging out sideways with each insatiable chomp. I turned away, unable to watch my once lovely feminine bitch, now transformed into a brutish, swollen savage. "Wow, that's freaky" she said. The technical phrase for we should run a few tests.

She did a thorough exam and in the end surmised two possibilities, Cushing's Disease or Acromegaly. Before she left, she drew blood that she would send off for testing, to give us a starting point.

Of course the instant she was gone, I got on the internet to research both Cushing's and Acromegaly. Neither was good and both could be terminal depending on the root cause.

And now there were three... In one week's time, three of my precious companions had come down with very serious disorders. Xelie's was fatal, as Cora's condition might well be. And poor Jambo, if her seizures began to get out of control... Lets just say, quality of life would need to be taken into consideration.

Why was this happening? The last two weeks had been downright unbelievable. Since childhood, I'd been told that God never delivers more challenges than an individual can handle. But I was beginning to think He must have me confused with someone else because I couldn't take much more.

It seemed that every day it was something, something big. In addition to Post Traumatic Stress Disorder I was developing another type of PTS -- Pre-Traumatic Stress Disorder. I was beginning to wake up each day fearful of what would happen next.

For years I had believed that when something extremely unusual or perfectly out of the ordinary occurred, that perhaps I should pay attention and take stock of what the powers that be might be trying to tell me. I suppose a dime store shrink might call this a coping mechanism. Whatever the case may be, I'd do my best to decipher the mystery.

Wake-up call… It's a giant wake-up call, I thought. All of the material things that had gone wrong since I'd returned from Colorado and before had been difficult and stressful, but I rolled with the punches and remained entrenched in my nose-to-the-grindstone world. I hadn't changed, not really.

Xelie had been the first alarm clock going off, she had made me stop and slow down. Apparently that wasn't enough, so the universe threw in Jambo, and just to be sure frosted the emotional meltdown cake with Cora's bizarre condition.

The prospect of losing three dogs in a short span of time was overwhelming. I sensed it proposed a message that could not be ignored. But what was it?

At that moment in time, the emotional rollercoaster I was riding made it impossible to see, but sitting here today, these are my thoughts.

Xelie was my heart dog, my last remaining companion who wasn't required to work to be a part of the family. Then there was Jambo, the most talented young dog I'd had, almost ever. She was the hope for the future. And finally Cora, she was my best all around Open dog that I was competing with right now.

Past. Present. Future. The analysis? The past, Xelie, was about to die, there was no doubt and no going back. The present, Cora, was at serious risk. And the future, Jambo, looked daunting but remained to be seen.

The truth was, the past was dead and there was nothing to do about it and whether I liked it or not, I needed to accept and move on. And the present, the present was at serious risk because I spent so much time worrying about the future and delving into the past. And the future remained to be seen, as is always the case in this mysterious journey we call life.

Amidst the emotional anguish that engulfed me that week, I wish I could have seen what I see sitting here now. Even through the pain, I would have appreciated the poetic nature with which this message had been delivered.

For the first time, at this moment, I thank God it hadn't been sent via English or human language. So commonplace a communiqué would not have penetrated in nearly as effective a manner.

It was a puzzle; it had taken time and effort to discern a possible meaning behind the events. And even now, there's no certainty that the message I received was the message that was intended. Or if there even is such a thing as a message or just one message. So I'll continue to think it over and mull possible meanings.

If the communication had been delivered in English I simply would have filed it away and moved on, down the same path, on to the next thing. Nothing would have changed, not really. I had thirteen years worth of material evidence to substantiate this fact, dating back to June 2001.

My life was in desperate need of a spiritual overhaul, and it was clear I wasn't getting there on my own. And here I thought I was so smart and insightful. How arrogant we can be without being aware we are such? A friend once said, "You don't know what you don't know". That would be me in a nutshell. Whether I liked it or not, this time the universe was going to make certain I awoke.

31.

That just doesn't happen...

I couldn't wait. Cora's condition was worsening by the minute. Five days to get the results of the initial blood work was simply too long. I phoned the Specialty clinic where Jambo's neurologist practiced. No matter how hard I pressed, the earliest possible appointment they'd agree to give me was the following Tuesday; and only if my primary vet called in to arrange it. Today was Thursday.

"I've never heard of an emergency Cushing's", the receptionist had said condescendingly. It took every ounce of self control to refrain from verbally battering this insensitive boob. The last thing I needed was a front desk dumbass interfering with Cora and her well being.

Long story short, my vet came to the rescue and arranged an appointment at Texas A&M Veterinary school for that very afternoon. As anyone who lives in Texas knows, A&M is renowned for superb veterinary care, handling some of the most complex and difficult cases.

I cancelled the remainder of my clients for the day. My Colorado traveling companion had been one of my calls. In lieu of her lesson she volunteered to join me at the clinic. I was an emotional wreck, but I couldn't bring myself to ask for help or support. She informed me she'd meet me there and that was that.

I loaded Cora in the car and was on my way, leaving Xelie behind with the run of the house. I had no idea that it would be eight hours later when I returned.

In order to get an appointment with a specialist, we had to first go through the emergency clinic. The doctor on duty was twelve, or at least he looked about that age although I'm sure he was older.

"She looks just fine" he responded after examining her. "Are you kidding?", I replied. Quickly my friend and I pulled up photographs on our i-Phones of the pre-syndrome Cora, beautiful and feminine, markedly different from the masculine pitbull mix lying on the floor in front of us.

The youngster couldn't discern that there had been any change, God help us. His sidekick, another student, had heard of acromegaly. Our "doctor" was surprised and asked what it was. It was then that I began my campaign for a specialist.

The two young men left the room to commiserate I'm sure. Some time later our infant doctor returned saying "It just doesn't happen, not to dogs". I proceeded to show him the spaces that had developed between her teeth as a result of the jaw bone increasing in size. And, of course, I flashed the pictures again and again.

Still skeptical, he would take Cora in the back, collect blood and urine and conducts tests. He took hold of her leash and off they went.

It had been a rough year for Cora, beginning with a pregnancy that had been uncomfortable almost from the very start. It was only the second or third week into her term when the panting had begun. Panting as if she was only days from delivering. This continued for almost six weeks. And when the time finally arrived for her babies to be born, her body would not cooperate. Cora's first pregnancy had ended in a C-section.

Not long after the puppies were weaned, as Cora was beginning to get back in shape, she lacerated her side, leaving underlying tissue and muscle exposed from her shoulder to the end of her rib cage, measuring four inches from top to bottom. Three layers of stitches and four abscesses later the wound finally healed.

But she wasn't herself, especially not at work. The powerful, aggressive Cora that I'd come to know and love over the years working sheep, was now slow, lackadaisical, and very inconsistent.

Something was wrong, I just didn't know what. At first I thought post-litter hormones, then residual pain and possible infection from the wound. But now, seven months later, these issues should have been resolved.

A vet and fellow stock dog competitor had taken note that Cora simply wasn't herself. At her suggestion, I began a hefty two-month course of antibiotics. I had completed that treatment just before taking off for the Colorado trial. And at the trial, Cora had worked marvelously, but had become strangely ravenous.

In retrospect I'm certain that all Cora's symptoms were due to the onset of Acromegaly. Now if only I could get to a Specialist, so we could move forward.

The waiting seemed interminable. Angie had been good company and an unobtrusive support. She was there for me, without making me feel as though I was weak or subpar. She had put her life aside for that day, to be there for me. I wondered if the roles were reversed, if I would do the same for her, or for anyone.

Finally, five hours into our visit, our doctor returned singing a brand new tune. Clearly, although he never would fully admit it, one of the specialists had looked at Cora and arrived at the same conclusion my vet and I had; the symptoms looked like Acromegaly. We were informed that she'd be on the specialist roster first up in the morning. Did I want to leave her overnight?

If I left her, I could keep my appointments the following morning. I could have worked and earned some money. I must be learning something I thought, because there was no choice. Cora would come home with me, and that was that.

It was almost 7pm when we started for home; Cora needed to be back by six. It was an hour and a half drive one way. I had two hours of chores in the morning and at least an hour and a half of chores when I returned home that evening. Needless to say I barely scraped together four hours of sleep that night.

I wasn't willing to lose another precious day with Xelie. It was 4:30 in the morning when she and Cora jumped into the backseat of the Honda. Back off to A&M we went.

As I drove I just couldn't believe what was happening. I caught sight of Cora and Xelie in the rearview mirror; the prospect of losing them both was almost more than I could bear.

Acromegaly was extremely rare, almost never occurring in a dog. Usually the result of a pituitary tumor or cancer of the mammary glands, either of which stimulates an overproduction of growth hormone. Thus the enlarged head, neck and body. If left untreated, everything would be affected, including her organs, until ultimately... You get the picture.

I'll say it again, this was almost unheard of. It was so extraordinarily strange and unusual, that it called up the question -- what are the powers that be trying to tell me? As I drank my coffee and drove down the highway, my mind came up empty; I had absolutely no idea.

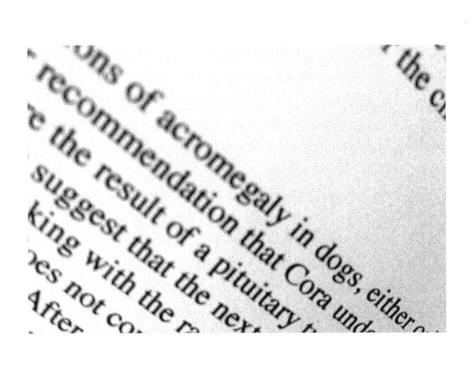

32.

A clue?

We arrived just before dawn. The doctor's sidekick from the day before greeted us at the door. He would take Cora to the back and prepare her for the Specialist to examine. I declined the offer to wait in the lobby, and headed back to the car to collect Xelie. This morning her sheep work would be replaced by a leisurely walk around campus.

An ethereal crimson hue heralded the imminent daybreak and saturated everything around us, the buildings, the sidewalks, even the grass, with an otherworldly feel. The parking lots were empty and it was still very quiet; the day here at A&M had not yet begun.

We started down a sidewalk, heading where, neither of us knew.

We were together and that was enough for me. And although my mind would dart now and again to the day's possible scenarios and future outcomes; for the most part, I was successful remaining in the present with Xelie.

She was enjoying our stroll, investigating a variety of not-in-the-country smells. The cushy, manicured lawns were entirely different from the sandy coastal grass she lorded over at home. And these cement sidewalks, hmmm...

Xelie had spent very little time in the city, I realized as we walked. But she was relaxed as could be; it was her confident nature. As we started back to the clinic, I began to sing a song. It was a song I had made up and sung since Xelie was very young. It was silly and not very complex, but it was her song and she knew it.

She trotted happily down the sidewalk, almost in rhythm to my screeching. A young student passed by us; he was clearly amused. Frankly, I didn't care if he thought I was a freak, I just kept singing as we continued on our way.

We'd been waiting in the lobby for an hour or more. The clinic was now open and abustle with activity. I had brought an assortment of food and a bowl for water, to keep Xelie as comfortable as possible in the event we were here for the entire day.

The same young man who had passed us on the sidewalk emerged from the back and called out my name. As I greeted him, we exchanged a smile of recognition; what are the chances that the only person that crossed our path that morning on our ethereal walk would be the same person to work with us that day?

He ushered us back into an exam room. It wasn't long before he returned with Cora and the lead Specialist on our case. Now <u>she</u> was a doctor, bright, knowledgeable and determined. For the first time in two days, I felt Cora was in good hands.

They had analyzed the urine and blood work taken the day before and had examined Cora thoroughly. The tests revealed Cora had a pre-diabetic condition that most probably resulted from her suspected

Acromegaly. Carbohydrates exacerbated the condition and thus Cora's ravenous desire for meat.

In addition, she had neurological changes to her back left leg. The in-house neurologist had not yet taken a look at her, so the cause was inconclusive. The worry of course, was that this symptom indicated an inoperable pituitary tumor.

They had already drawn and frozen blood to be shipped out for a growth hormone test – very rare, only two labs in the country performed the test. And results would not be forthcoming for at least five business days or more.

Xelie lay on the cool floor not far from Cora as the doctors and I discussed the next course of action. Both dogs were comfortable and, as always, in the moment. I don't know if Cora was happy that Xelie was there, but I know Xelie was. Cora was an integral member of her pack, after all. And although they were not as close as she and Nell, Xelie was committed, as always, to caring for any member of her group -- myself included.

The diagnostic procedures that were now on the table would have required me to rob a bank, maybe more than one. My financial resources were taxed already and another $4000 MRI, in addition to everything we'd already done, was next to impossible.

I began my campaign – this was a learning institution after all, and Cora's case was extremely rare. I requested that inquiries be made as to whether or not there were research funds available to assist with the costs.

The doctor nodded, having already had the thought. She informed me someone was already on board to underwrite a CT Scan should we go that route. The next steps were a neurological exam and an ultrasound of her abdomen to determine if any reproductive cancer was evident.

Now I'll save you all the details and the meticulous descriptions of the emotional rollercoaster I rode that day. Suffice to say, four hours later, we'd determined that the neurological changes to Cora's leg were due to an old injury, not brain malfunction. The ride finally came to a sudden stop when the ultrasound revealed cysts on both Cora's ovaries.

This could be plenty, the young Internist explained, to cause the hyperactive production of growth hormone. Simple enough, I thought, we'll spay her and if the symptoms subside, then in all likelihood we've discovered the cause.

It was Friday, one week to the day from when Jambo had convulsed for hours. It was ten days following Xelie's trip to the Specialty Clinic and the oncologist's confirmed diagnosis of lymphoma. Finally, today, in the midst of all the drama, the best possible scenario had emerged. There was hope. Hope amidst chaos and crisis. It was possible this could be a simple fix.

Sitting here now I realize the journey I was on with Cora offered up yet another bit of food for thought. In the midst of what appears to be disastrous and catastrophic, if one quiets the mind and looks beyond the drama, if one is aware of the worst possible scenarios, yet isn't enveloped by the emotion of them... In this quiet strangely detached frame of mind, a freedom emerges. Freedom from preconceived notions. And when the shackles of presumption fall away, sometimes an effortless and uncomplicated solution will emerge.

I don't know if this was exactly what happened that day from the Internist's point of view, but it was from mine. They had done the ultrasound to determine whether mammary cancer was indicated; a scenario almost as serious as a pituitary tumor in terms of recovery and cost.

Instead, we found something none of us expected. It was a gift even more rare than an Acromegalic dog. Simple ovarian cysts. An unheard of presentation for Acromegaly, but a possible one. Compared to the fatal alternatives, it was a gift for which I was wholly grateful. I could afford a spay and delighted at the hope that Cora would recover.

The hiccup? There was no one available in all of A&M's veterinary school to perform a simple neutering procedure. It would be a week or more. Cora couldn't wait. To my eye, her head had grown since we'd arrived that morning.

It wasn't a spay to be done by just anyone. It was imperative that every last bit of tissue be removed so there was no chance of regrowth. I called the reproductive vet who had done Cora's C-Section, and two C-sections prior to hers. The doctor couldn't do the procedure that day, but would be happy to take care of it on Monday.

I made the appointment, hoping that Cora's head wouldn't explode in the two interim weekend days between now and then.

33.

A finite existence

Despite Cora's drama, that Saturday morning I kept my promise to Xelie and out to work sheep we went. She loved our new routine. I kept asking myself why had I waited? Why had I waited so long to make the extra effort? Why had the communication between us that had once come so naturally, fallen discarded by the wayside for so many years?

Truth is, I was too busy. Too busy with work. I had every moment of every day scheduled so as not to waste time. Why couldn't I see that in having absolutely no time to spare, I was actually squandering precious moments?

I was too busy controlling everything and everyone. I was a trainer after all. It was my job. I was so busy telling everyone what to do, that I couldn't hear over my own voice. And my voice had gotten so loud in my own head, I couldn't hear what silence had to offer. I had forgotten about listening, not only to my dogs, but to my inner voice and what the universe was trying to tell me.

I was too busy believing that I always knew best. My intentions were good and I meant no harm, but bottom line is this was undeniably arrogant. So arrogant in fact, that I'd forgotten to pay attention to the beauty that surrounded me. The life. The variety. I was nothing in comparison to the grandeur this planet displayed. Arrogance, an illusion for the spiritually unconscious...

But thanks to Xelie, life for everyone, the dogs and myself included, was beginning to improve. I had a long way to go, but at least I was changing roads to begin a fresh journey.

I have no idea if Xelie was aware or intended to be such a tremendous influence; or if some greater power was simply working through her? Or if it was neither? Or if it was both? Or if it was something beyond my infantile imaginations?

In the end, the question is inconsequential. What's relevant is the effect, the journey and the ultimate outcome. All this, just by realizing Xelie's life was finite, a fact that I somehow, at some level, had chosen to deny. A fact accentuated by all of the other terribly challenging events.

Death would come, it would come to all of us. There would be an end, and from that moment forward there would be no changing any aspect or path we had taken. The ending is what makes the beginning and the middle, and all the choices in between, count. If there were no ending, we'd have forever to make things right, or not...

A fact that, when embraced, has the power to inspire the very best in a person. A finite existence, how brilliant a plan!

34.

Beds fit for a Queen

Cora's head did not explode that weekend but by Monday morning I was quite relieved to get the spay underway. At least we'd have an answer; at least that's what I hoped.

Xelie joined us for the trip into town, as now was the custom. She poked her nose at the window, her message was clear. I hit the button, rolling it down so she could luxuriate in the scent-uous breeze. Cora sat on the seat beside her, panting, eyes bulging, indifferent to the open window.

Before long we had arrived. It was too warm to leave Xelie in the car, not that I would have left her even if it had been cool. My reproductive vet got her first look at Cora, amazed at the physical changes she displayed. Before long, she took her in the back and we went on our way. We would return that afternoon to pick up Cora, once the operation was complete.

It was my day off if such a thing exists. In actuality, Mondays were my day to take care of bookkeeping, banking, grocery shopping and any number of other errands. To rephrase, Mondays I am closed to the public.

I added another errand to my to-do list that day. Xelie needed a new bed. I had already purchased two beds for her since I'd been informed she was sick. Not that there hadn't been dog beds available in the house, but they were all border collie size and, like the swim pools, they just weren't quite large enough. At least that's what I thought.

Two weeks before, I'd bought an extra large pillow style bed at Tractor Supply, but it had proven to be too puffy and squishy for Xelie's taste, she looked unsteady as she traversed her way atop it. It had laid on the dining room floor, unused, since she'd taken that first spin.

It was clear Xelie needed something solid, yet comfy. Memory foam would be just perfect, I concluded. I had made a special trip to Petco my next available opportunity. They carried a wide selection of luxurious beds.

Which would she like? There were four contenders that I had placed on the floor. There was no way to know without trying them myself. I stretched out that day, moving from one to another, trying to imagine which one Xelie would prefer.

I had narrowed it down to two. They were both memory foam, and both quite snazzy. They were eight times the price of any bed I had ever purchased, but Xelie was worth it. She had always been thin and now, with her illness, she was losing even more weight. Truth is I would have paid double their cost to make her happy and comfortable.

I had made the final selection based on looks alone as they were both equally comfortable. Xelie had graciously posed for a photo-op when I presented her this bed fit for a queen but, after that, I rarely saw her use it. She preferred the hard cold tile. I couldn't believe it.

Xelie enjoyed the windy ride to Petco this Monday, the Monday of Cora's spay. I'd switched cars and taken my truck, as I could lock the doors with the engine and air conditioning running. This was the vehicle for running errands with Xelie.

I purchased the other memory foam contender that I'd left behind the week before. Xelie will surely like this one, I thought. It was flatter, with no rise at the ends.

I set the magnificent new cushy mat on the floor and asked Xelie to give it a whirl. She dropped down atop it, surprisingly unenthused. I whipped out my camera to commemorate the moment. She looked at me "not another picture", then turned away.

Before long she settled back on the cool tile nearby. Okay, she just doesn't want a bed, I thought. You see I had tried everything I could think of, I had moved them to various places in the house, under air conditioning vents, out of the AC, in the living room, the kitchen, the dining room. She couldn't have communicated more clearly that she preferred the floor.

At least to these three new beds… There was one thing I'd forgotten. Something essential to Xelie. Something she'd shown me over and over was important to her. Something that in the not-too-distant future would become crystal clear.

Cora, 4 AM

35.

The incredible shrinking head

I left Xelie at home that afternoon when I went to pick up Cora. She was showing some fatigue from the errands of the day and I wanted to be certain Cora would arrive home without complications to her incision.

We were in the clinic lobby; my vet was explaining that the procedure had been a success, and that none of the tissue appeared cancerous, when one of the staff emerged from the back with a dog. They approached and handed me the leash. It was Cora; I barely recognized her.

Not to be repetitive, but her head looked even larger than when I'd dropped her off that morning. I'm not sure what I expected, a miracle I

143

guess. Somehow I must have imagined Cora's head would begin to shrink the instant the offending ovaries had been removed.

She was out of it, the anesthesia still at play. She could walk, but looked a little unsteady like a drunk. I loaded her in the car and started for home. The bathroom adjacent to my bedroom would be her recovery quarters. I'd prepared it with a fresh bowl of water and the new bed I'd purchased for Xelie from Tractor Supply.

Cora settled in nicely, happy to fall asleep atop the brand new bed. At least someone liked it, I thought. Leaving on only a nightlight, I quietly closed the door behind me so she could be alone, undisturbed, to rest and recover.

Cora did not join the pack that evening for free time outside. Xelie lorded over the others as I left to check on Cora a number of times throughout the evening.

And all through the night... It was 4 a.m. when I entered the dimly nightlit room. Half asleep, I reached to pet Cora's head; it felt different, flatter, smaller. I quickly turned on the overhead lights. Cora blinked back at me, her eyes weren't bulging. I wanted to celebrate and throw a party right then and there. It was a miracle. I was more than hopeful the procedure had worked.

Amazing what a little neuter can do. I thought of a few men in my life that would benefit from a little male-spay of their own.

I returned to my bedroom, announcing the good news to my house-dog cast. I'm not sure they understood what I was saying, but they seemed happy that I was happy. I crawled back into bed and closed my eyes, relieved and grateful at the prospect of a second chance with Cora.

photo by Bob Degus

36.

Whatever you think...

We were into our third week now since Xelie had been confirmed with Lymphoma. If only there were a solution for her as simple as the one we'd discovered for Cora. In the knowledge that no such panacea existed, Xelie and I made the best of every moment.

She was beginning to lose weight, in spite of the fact her buffet was growing. But her appetite was still within acceptable limits. Her eyes were bright and engaging, and her energy surprisingly good for the condition she was in.

Working sheep was still on the top of her list. So every day without fail, we kept to the schedule and, first up, headed out in the cool morning light to match wits with the herd.

Now the average person may believe that sheep are pea-brained morons with only a limited number of neurons at their dimwitted disposal, but that is certainly not the case. Don't get me wrong, Einstein they're not, but they do have thoughts and opinions and the ability to process information.

Perhaps in their world, we humans are the ignorant ones. Perhaps intelligence is variable, not concrete, and dependent on the parameters of measurement, nothing more.

Philosophizing aside, the fact of the matter is that when dogs come in contact with sheep, the sheep almost invariably form an opinion about the dog. Is it strong? Is it weak? Is it inexperienced? Is it hunting? It's amazing how quickly sheep can discover a hole in the dog's character or training.

Such was the case with Xelie. She had been so good, moving the sheep methodically and calmly. But clearly the herd was becoming aware that Xelie's condition was compromised. And being the opportunists they are, they began to take advantage.

It was in one such instance that I had to laugh. One of the older more savvy ewes was beginning to think she didn't have to move at all, whether Xelie was there or not, especially if the grass was green and lush in the area she was passing.

After going back for her more than once, Xelie was just plain fed-up. Quicker than you could blink an eye, she grabbed that ewe and tossed her to the ground as if to say, "Just because I'm old and sick, don't think I still can't take you!"

I couldn't help myself, as sick as it sounds, I was chuckling out loud as I extricated the ewe's thigh from Xelie's jaws. There was no real damage, except to the sheep's ego I suppose. I couldn't blame Xelie. Word was out, she was not the dog she used to be, that she was older and much weaker. If Xelie was going to work them, she needed to make a point. And that she did.

As we continued moving the group down into the field, I harkened back to the memories of young Xelie taking down sheep in the most violent of manners. I had tried everything I knew to stop the behavior. But you don't know, what you don't know.

I had never tried one on one, equal to equal, direct communication with Xelie. I wondered if I had sat quietly with her and asked the obvious question, why, why did she want to attack them? And if I'd had a quiet enough mind to hear her response... I wondered if together we could have arrived at a solution.

Being intuitive or psychic comes much more naturally to dogs than it does to most humans. Time and time again in the process of training, I've had to remind dogs to wait until I speak the command, and not go when I think it.

Which begged the question right then and there, as Xelie and I pushed the sheep deeper into the field. What had I been thinking years ago when I was training Xelie? It doesn't take more than one good sheep assault to instill a vivid image in your brain from that point forward. And from the very beginning the breeders had warned that Picards were notorious for being hard on sheep.

Had I been thinking about and picturing the possibilities of attack? I had consciously guarded against that, so I must have had a grizzly picture in my head. Was it possible that, all those years, Xelie had received this image at the forefront of my mind, and acted upon it with the mistaken belief that it was the desired and expected behavior.

Had I contributed to the demise of her sheepherding career without even knowing it? I'm certain I had. The realization was devastating.

And enlightening. There was nothing I could do, at this moment in time, to change all the years Xelie had lost, all the years she was denied doing what she loved most.

But from here forward, I could be aware. Aware of what I was thinking. Be aware of my expectations and the pictures I held in my mind. Be open to the fact that communication does indeed exist between humans and animals; that they deserve the respect to be considered and heard.

And know that thoughts do have power. Whatever you think, if you think it clearly and intensely enough, whatever you think, you can think into existence. The implications were almost beyond comprehension.

From that point forward, I committed to adding these invaluable insights to both my training regimen and personal life.

Thank you, Xelie.

37.

A last hoorah

Xelie loved her new life. She happily greeted my clients as they came and went from the house. And now, she wanted the same freedom to come and go. More and more I'd let her outside during business hours to join me and visit with my friends and students.

I had no idea what a social animal Xelie was at heart. Why I was surprised, I'm not sure. She had always introduced herself to any new dog that had entered our pack, either permanent or temporary. She'd been outgoing from the time we'd brought her home from Austria.

But she'd never been exposed to many people outside the immediate family. Perhaps because she and Lucy had similarities in appearance, I had subconsciously attributed Lucy's hair trigger aggressive tendencies to Xelie as well.

Whatever the case, Xelie was delighted to visit; a Walmart greeter couldn't have held a candle to her enthusiasm.

The picture now was almost complete. All those years in the bedroom, looking out the window, wishing and hoping for more. Now, now she was living the dream. I believe these were the happiest days of Xelie's life.

She not only had sheep and the run of the house, but was free to be out during business hours to visit and thrive. She'd nudge people with a hello, run the fence barking for sheep. She'd dunk in the swim pool, then get out and dig her nose joyfully in the sand. I hope heaven equals what the last few weeks had delivered.

On Thursday June 26th, my eldest group of sheep, sheep I had brought with me from California, were loaded on a trailer. My friend, Angie, had more greener pastures than she knew what to do with. She had volunteered to take the old ewes so they could live out their lives work free. It seemed like the best thing for them and removed them from my feed bill.

So on that day as they headed out the driveway on their way to full retirement, we said goodbye to the sheep that had known Xelie from the very beginning.

Xelie's decline first began on Friday June 27th. Down the hill in the pasture she still loved working her sheep, but her endurance was waning. Work periods were getting shorter, while pool time was getting longer. She stood in the water, droplets dripping from her beard, staring back at the sheep, wanting to return; she had the will to work but the energy escaped her.

Saturday was her very last trip working down in that part of the field. We had finished a short session and had been quite some time in the pool. It was clear, in spite of the fact that she wanted to continue, she simply could not. I studied her, unsure she had the energy to make the trek back up the hill to the house.

She was comfortably soaking when I discretely made an exit. I'll drive the truck down and give her a ride back up, that was my intent. But before I'd reached the top of the hill, she had started on her way after me. She reminded me of an Indian, proud and strong. Energy or not, she was going to make it to the top without anyone's help.

We only worked sheep in the upper field and on the top of the hill after that. Up to that point, she had always been agreeable to stopping and resting when I had asked her to do so. But something had changed and now, now she didn't want to quit, even when I tugged on her collar. I know she knew her days of sheep work were almost over.

Xelie was going for broke now. It was later in the morning that Saturday, she had taken a post-herding nap, and now she wanted to be outside with me. In the past three weeks, my Saturday morning regulars had gotten to know Xelie and grown to love her quirky personality.

She greeted everyone, but made it her business to keep track of where I was going. Before long, I headed to my little upper field, to give another lesson. Xelie trotted beside me, then in front of me, beating me to the gate leading to the field and the sheep beyond. Her communication was unmistakable. I explained that I had a lesson to give and that she'd have to wait outside the gated pasture.

I wasn't long into my lesson when Xelie made her opinion known. She ran the fence, bouncing and barking. I could barely believe this was the same dog I almost had to drive up the hill earlier that morning. Maybe the end wasn't so near, I hoped and I wished…

Sadly, not all our wishes come true. Xelie had delighted in her last hoorah, but by Sunday it was clear we were entering a new phase.

Xelie's last work.

38.

The homestretch

I have video of Xelie's last work. It was the only video I had taken, and I had taken a few, that I had put a date on, declaring it was Sunday, the last Sunday in June.

My lessons had begun at 7:30 that morning. It was a light day with only two dogs scheduled. Several clients had needed to cancel, and I hadn't bothered to schedule anyone in their place. I could feel time was getting short and I wanted to spend as much of it as I could with Xelie.

Before I knew it, my lessons were over and Xelie and I were walking down the driveway to lock the gate behind my clients as they left.

By now, I had many pictures of Xelie, but that morning, I realized I didn't have any of the two of us together. Over the years my husband had been the photographer. He had all the old photos and I just couldn't remember...

We headed back inside; I grabbed up my phone and took aim. I shot seven pictures of Xelie and me together, my emotional rollercoaster, riding up and down between joy and grief, evident in the sequence of shots.

And Xelie the constant, content, happy, the stabilizer; to her mind, we were together, and it was another day to be lived to the fullest.

It was not long after that we went back outside and onto the sheep. They were up the hill beside the house, perfect for Xelie. Off she trotted, and on went my camera the last Sunday in June.

The last Sunday in June was the first night Xelie and I slept in the living room. The stairway to my bedroom was just too much and I feared even if she could climb the steps she might not be able to get down them in the morning.

Xelie liked the living room and free reign in the house, so sleeping downstairs didn't much seem to phase her. I didn't know if she knew she'd never again see the bedroom where she'd spent so much time over so many years. Maybe she wouldn't care even if she knew.

By Monday there was no doubt, we were on the homestretch whether we liked it or not. Xelie's appetite had been declining, requiring more and more creativity in the menu and more supplicant begging on my part. She needed to eat at least enough food to mitigate the potential stomach irritation that the steroids could cause.

If I'd kept a diary I could have told you exactly when, but suffice to say, at some point in the few days prior, Xelie had told me in no uncertain terms that she didn't want to eat. No matter what delicacy I presented her, she had turned her head in refusal.

In a panic, knowing that to stop steroids suddenly can be lethal in and of itself, I had shoved enough food down her throat to neutralize any ill-effect from the pill. It was the only time I can remember, almost ever, Xelie being angry and it was directed at me. I could almost hear her say "How dare you?" She was humiliated.

What happened to mutual respect and communication? I had manhandled her. Don't misunderstand, I had in no way injured her or even come close to such a thing. I had manhandled her spirit. And there was no doubt I had completely let her down.

I apologized. Profusely. And then I had the conversation with her that I should have had in the first place, before forcing food into her. I explained that I couldn't just stop giving her these pills, even if I wanted to, not without serious ramifications.

I explained that I was not trying to torture her and that I could understand if she was beginning to feel like she no longer wanted to eat. I made clear this was part of her illness and that I was sorry she didn't feel good.

I then offered a solution. If she would agree to eat just enough so that I could give her the pills, then I wouldn't ask her to eat any more if she didn't want to.

From that point forward, every morning and every evening, she ate just enough to safely take her pills. It's amazing how much you can accomplish with a simple conversation.

For more than three weeks now, since the initial diagnosis, I had been giving Xelie powerful supplements to help her feel the best that she could for as long as she could. I'd dissolve them in water and administer them in her mouth through a small syringe. She didn't like it, but it didn't piss her off like the food incident had.

She'd been a good sport. But now the supplements had done all they were going to do so, out of respect for Xelie, I stopped them all together.

It was Monday morning and a day for our usual end of the week errands. Xelie wanted to join me as she had almost every time I'd taken a car trip in the last three weeks. I couldn't refuse her.

The trip into town was much more taxing than it had been in the past. Xelie still enjoyed the vast array of smells the open car window provided, but it was much more difficult for her to actually stand, balance and stretch her nose out of the truck. She spent much of the time just sitting on the seat letting the wind wash over her.

As I watched her in the rearview mirror, I thought to myself this could very well be her last trip in the truck. Tears welled up in my eyes. I didn't want her to go. I'd said it over and over as I began each day and ended each day, and many times in between. I'd said it since that first Monday my vet had diagnosed her.

The last three weeks had been splendid, which is hardly a grand enough word to express what the time had meant to me. I had known the end would come, but had attempted to live in the moment like Xelie, and enjoy as many seconds, minutes, hours and days as I could without reflecting on the inevitable…

And now, here we were, on the homestretch. I did my best to wipe away the tears. Xelie had given me so much, not just in the last three weeks but in the whole of her life. It was my turn to give back, to be strong and to help with her transition.

39.

The final days

It was Tuesday, the first day of July. With the holiday looming on the horizon, I had made arrangements to take Cora in a little early to have her stitches removed. I had no intention of bringing Xelie on the heels of our trip the day before. But she insisted, she absolutely did not want to be left behind.

I pulled the Honda to the back door and helped Xelie into the back seat. Cora leapt in after her. As we made our way into town, I kept an eye on Xelie. The delight she had come to derive from a car ride was no longer evident. She just leaned up against the seat, biding her time.

Xelie joined us in the clinic as the doctor removed Cora's stitches.

The incision had healed nicely and the horrific acromegalic symptoms Cora had suffered had subsided. As I spoke with the vet, I couldn't help but notice Xelie, lying down for most of the visit, not unfriendly, but not her usual outgoing self.

Before long we were back on the road. Reaching home, I pulled in the driveway and parked just where I always did, just inside the gate. I helped Xelie out of the car. Cora bounded down the driveway, headed to the kennels and the house beyond.

Xelie was moving more slowly than normal. I had walked on ahead of her and then stopped beside the kennels waiting for her to catch up. It was at that moment I realized what a terrible oversight I'd made.

Xelie was about halfway between the car and the house when she stopped, unable to continue any further. If I had just pulled the car up to the house; what was I thinking?

It was clear she would not make it inside of her own volition. First I apologized for being an imperceptive ignoramus, then I picked her up and started toward the house. She didn't seem to mind, she knew she needed the help.

The last time I'd carried Xelie in my arms was when she was a young pup, with her whole life ahead of her. Now, at thirteen years old, I was carrying her with almost her whole life behind her.

The illness had taken its toll and she was only fifty pounds or less. I brought her inside and put her on the carpet where her feet could get traction. She stood there for a moment, very weak, then lay down on the floor to rest.

The downturn had been quick and, as much as I would have liked to believe otherwise, it was obvious there wasn't a lot of time left.

I wanted Xelie to die at home, in a place that she loved, a place that was familiar. I absolutely did not want her ending to be heralded by a stressful, uncomfortable car ride, and finalized in a cold unfamiliar clinic.

I didn't know how much longer she had, but I was keenly aware we were headed into a holiday weekend, clinics would be closed and vets on vacation. I placed a call to my vet to confirm whether or not she would be available through the weekend should Xelie need assistance in the transition.

As was her custom over many a holiday, my vet was going to be out of town. She was kind enough, however, to give me the name and phone number of another mobile vet who, in the past, had assisted a client of hers in this way.

I stared at the new phone number, feeling almost as if making the call would cause the worst to happen. The truth was, it was going to happen regardless of whether or not I placed the call. I had no way of knowing whether Xelie would need help but, in the event she did, I wanted to be prepared.

I dialed the number and introduced myself to the gentleman vet on the other end of the line. I explained the circumstance with Xelie and asked if he would be available should the need arise. He was very kind and reassured me he would help, not to worry.

It was an emotional call to make, but when it was finished I felt very relieved. Xelie had looked after me for so many years; now I needed to look after her.

Xelie rested for a number of hours that afternoon regaining enough energy to join the pack that evening for free-time out. Exploring the yard and the smells that resided there had been so commonplace and easy for her in the past, but tonight was different. Tonight Xelie spent much less time than usual roaming and much more time perched atop her sandy throne.

As always, Nell was nearby. The two were never very far apart. I used to joke that Nell was an island, independent of the typical hierarchical constraints. She was Xelie's favorite, and being under the wing of the alpha, no one even considered messing with her.

I wondered if Nell knew that Xelie would not be with us much longer? I wondered what her life would be like once Xelie was gone? I wondered if she'd remain the untouchable island she had been for the past thirteen years?

As I watched the two of them together, I vowed to make sure, when all was said and done, that I would take as good care of Nell as Xelie had for all these years. And if anyone even thought to mess with Nell, they'd have to go through me first.

But most of all I wondered if Nell would be happy without her best friend? I worried about it in fact. Nell was now thirteen as well, and showing her age. Only several months before, in the middle of April, I had returned home one day to find Nell, on the floor, surrounded by vomit, unable to walk.

A trip to the specialty clinic revealed a diagnosis of vestibular disease, "old dog" syndrome. Most often caused by a disturbance deep in the inner ear, we had been able to treat Nell and she had recovered, almost entirely.

But I worried; the stress of losing her dearest companion, Xelie, might be enough to send her cascading down. I worried it would be like an old married couple, when the first one passes away, the second frequently is soon to follow.

So much for living in the moment that evening... I took Xelie in the house a little earlier that night than was the usual custom. It had been a long day and we'd already overdone it.

photo by Bob Degus

40.

Sue's goodbye...

It was the first night in all these weeks that Xelie was visibly uncomfortable. She was restless much of the night, but much worse than that, the sparkle that had always shone bright in her eyes was not just dim, it was now completely gone.

I texted Auntie Sue the next morning that Xelie didn't have long. She and Xelie had been good friends and I wanted to give her an opportunity to visit if she so wished.

It wasn't yet 9 a.m. when Sue arrived. We reached for each other, and the moment we embraced, the tears flooded forth. Life without Xelie, we could barely imagine.

I showed Sue into the house. Xelie was lying in the dining room, on the tile, not far from the two luxurious beds that rested unused nearby. As Sue bent down to sit beside her, I stepped back out the door, allowing them some privacy to say their goodbyes.

Sue spent almost two hours with Xelie that morning as I gave lessons outside. And when she was ready to leave, she gave me a big tearful hug goodbye.

It was after 2pm when I finally came in for the day. I'd been checking on Xelie regularly, and although subdued, she seemed stable.

It's somewhat of a blur, but I believe I had just sat down for lunch when I checked my phone for messages. There was a voicemail and a text from Sue. I looked at the text first. "Call me", it read.

Then the voice message, Sue was hysterical. "Something terrible has happened", she needed me to call.

Sue lost her son that day. She had been on my dining room floor with Xelie saying her goodbyes, only moments before her son was saying his final farewell.

Later she told me, that morning she had gone to the breakfast nook window to take a break from the emotion of it all. As she looked out over the pasture, watching us work dogs below, something came over her. Standing there at the window, she faced directly toward her son's house who lived only a mile or two away.

Standing there at that window, she had been overcome with this intense feeling at the exact moment her son drew his last breath. She had assumed it was grief over Xelie that had washed over her that day. It was grief to be sure, but not just for Xelie.

Just less than two weeks before, our friend, Red, a sheepherding icon, had passed away at the formidable age of ninety. As is her nature, Sue had helped both him and his family with his transition from living independently on his twenty acre ranch in the country, to moving into an assisted living facility in the city of Austin.

She extended herself even further, by offering to clean and fix up the ranch that was in a state of disrepair, so that it could be sold, or so she could buy it herself. It was an agreement that worked for Red, his family and for Sue.

It was there, at Red's home in the country, on the morning of Saturday June 21st, that Sue had noticed something new. Red birds. Not just one, but many of them. Red had loved birds and had a number of feeders to attract. But not until that morning had Sue seen Red birds.

She thought to herself, he is gone. And she was right. Red died that morning, the same morning the red birds appeared to Sue on the porch of his former home.

She had lost two people dear to her, in less than two weeks. And in each instance she had felt their parting.

My heart ached for Sue as we spoke that afternoon. I knew the grief I felt, and how difficult it was for me on the precipice of Xelie's death. I couldn't imagine what it must be like for her to lose her son of over forty years.

Death, so much death... What was the message, what could it mean?

41.

Xelie rallies

It had been a long draining day, that Wednesday, July 2nd. Xelie had slept almost all of our waking hours. And the times she'd awakened, she had hardly been able to stand, much less walk, even the shortest distance. At least sleeping was peaceful, I thought. And frankly, I didn't think she'd do much of anything else until she finally slipped away.

But Xelie had never been typical, in any way, shape, or form. Unpredictable and surprising were two traits integral in her life. And today was no different, it was, after all, another day of her life.

It was the end of the afternoon, and time for the pack to go

Xelie rose to her feet.

outside. I had just let the last dog out, when I returned to the house. Xelie rose to her feet, fairly stable. She stood in the living room, looking at me. "What?" she asked. It was a miracle.

I quickly took a photo, then another, and another. I think maybe the only way I could believe it was to see it on my phone.

And she was hungry. It was more than a miracle!

Xelie ate a full plate of rotisserie chicken, a few strips of bacon and a rib bone that night. And I thought I'd never see her eat much of anything again. Everyone had always said "When they stop eating, that's when…" You know the rest.

Poor Sue, maybe I had sent out a false alarm -- and on this day, the day of her son's death. Or maybe, maybe her visit with Xelie prepared her for her son's death, if one can ever be prepared for that. Whatever the case, this was a different dog this evening than she'd been this morning and throughout the day.

Maybe Xelie had more time than I thought. She had just eaten enough to feed an army; that must mean something, right? I was clinging to hope, and Xelie was clinging to life.

Completely on her own, Xelie made her way outside and pottied. Then headed directly to the sandy spot that I called her throne. She lorded over her kingdom and her pack even that evening of the day I presumed would be her last.

The dogs raced about, chasing and playing, still garnering Xelie all the respect she deserved. And Xelie reveled in the beautiful twilight that shown over them that evening.

42.

The shutdown begins

It was Thursday, July 3rd. Xelie had slept through the night much more comfortably than the night before but by morning she was markedly weaker. It was the first morning in days she refused every item presented on her buffet. I knew the end was near, but it was not yet here, and Xelie needed her pill.

I stuffed the tablet into a large piece of hamburger and broke my promise. I pushed it down her throat. Xelie was not at all pleased. I reminded her of our agreement. We both had gone back on our word. We renewed our vow so to speak, that Xelie would eat just enough for the pill and that I would not force food upon her.

And from that point forward, until the moment she passed from this life, leaving her beautiful wheaten body behind, Xelie ate just enough food to neutralize the pills.

I was done with lessons by noon that Thursday. And the dogs that were in for training? Well, they'd just have to wait. The rest of this day was for Xelie.

Xelie's sparkle had returned, even though her strength had not. She was very unsteady on her feet. I helped her outside so she could potty. Xelie loved being outside, even now, even when she could barely stand.

It was a hot day, one of the very first of this summer. The mercury had risen beyond 90 degrees. As a rule in Texas, from June forward until the end of September or October, anything below a hundred degrees is considered a cold front. This summer had been quite the exception, with most days rising only into the temperate eighties.

Just under four weeks prior, when I discovered Xelie was sick, I had dreaded the summer inferno to come, empathizing with how difficult it would be for someone with an illness such as hers.

But thus far this summer, it had been miraculously cool. I fancied that Xelie had willed it so, and so it was. She had always hated the extreme heat that was all too commonplace here for three to four months out of the year.

It had become her habit during the hot months, to stand on the back porch just outside the window, look in, and bark her request to enter the house and escape the dreadful sun.

But there was no need for that, not this summer, at least not so far. Until today... Today it was just plain hot. Xelie and I returned inside to the respite of the cool AC, where she came to rest in one of her favorite spots on the dining room floor.

Sue returned that afternoon for yet another visit. She wanted to see Xelie, and I hoped I could be a sympathetic ear should she need to talk. We sat on the dining room floor, each on opposite sides of Xelie, and spoke for hours.

It was a conversation unlike any Sue and I had ever shared. It was the second time Xelie had inspired and prompted a deep philosophical conversation, the first being the night of the storm, with Angie, when she was initially diagnosed.

The truth is, over the past three weeks and four days, I had participated in more meaningful conversations, with more friends, than I had engaged in I can't remember how many years. The seeds Xelie planted had grown into food for thought, thought that, in all probability, would not have been inspired without her imminent sacrifice on the horizon.

As Sue and I sat on the floor that afternoon, stroking Xelie and talking, I couldn't help but notice... You see the steroids that Xelie had been taking caused her to pant more than the average dog might. Today was no different.

Xelie lay on the floor between us, mouth slightly open, panting and revealing her gums, which were fading from a lively sweet pink to an almost greyish white. As Sue and I spoke of death, Xelie's death had begun. It wouldn't be a bad way to go, book-ended by the two people who loved her the most, I thought.

White gums or not, Xelie was alive and alert when Sue left that day. She was still resting on the dining room floor when I set the dogs free for the evening time out. I was unsure whether Xelie had the strength to join them. She somehow got to her feet; her answer was "yes".

Xelie stepped out of the screened in porch and down two steps onto the sidewalk. She was fragile and a trifle unsteady. Once she looked stable, I headed to one of the swim pools to fill it with water.

I glanced back at Xelie just in time to see her crash forward; head first, she hit the sidewalk with a thunk. Oh my God. I ran and gathered her up. I'm still unsure if she simply collapsed or if one of the dogs accidentally knocked into her, sending her helplessly to the ground.

But neither scenario was good. Xelie had retained her dignity up to now. And I was going to see to it she retained it to the end. I scooped her up in my arms and took her back inside.

It wasn't much more than an hour later when substantial storm clouds appeared, looming dark, approaching from the east. And then the wall of wind, cool and strong, began to kick up dust.

I'll put the dogs up before the storm hits, I thought. And that's what I did. Only the storm never actually arrived, it simply delivered cool refreshing temperatures. Our high for the day, exceeding the 95 degree mark, had now dropped to below eighty.

I stepped out onto the back porch overlooking the pasture where Xelie and I had worked bright and early those many wonderful mornings. Xelie loved sitting on the porch. It offered a perfect vantage point to keep watch over her kingdom. She and her best friend Nell would begin each day in this very spot.

Thanks to the storm, the storm that never fully arrived, the porch was now cool, offering a breathtaking view of the sunset to come. It had been days since Xelie had been able to climb the steps to this very spot.

What would Xelie want on an evening such as this? She had been absent from the pack that late afternoon for almost the first time in her entire tenure as alpha. I wanted to give her something; something she would enjoy, and remember, if that's possible for a creature who lives moment by moment.

As I stood there, on the porch, on top of the hill, gazing out to the west, I knew. Xelie would like it out here tonight, I knew she would.

It was a wooden deck, dusty with dog prints and hard, very hard. And by now, there was not much flesh between Xelie's bones and the ground. To be comfortable, she'd need a bed.

Well we all know what she thought of the memory foam I had purchased. Besides, the porch was dirty. I grabbed an old bed from the screened in porch. That's where used beds that had been soiled beyond resuscitation were placed before they reached the point of no return and were discarded altogether.

I threw a clean blanket atop it and placed it on the back porch in a spot with a perfect view of the field. I went back inside where Xelie now waited, curious as to what was coming next. I scooped her up in my arms and carried her out onto the porch where I laid her gently atop the old bed.

I invited Nell out to join us. Xelie beamed. She looked happier than words can describe. Here she was, in her favorite spot, gazing out over her favorite view, with Nell her favorite friend, her most loyal companion that she loved through and through. Here they could spend these last precious moments together. Not only had I figured out exactly what would make her happy that evening, but I'd finally figured out, as inadvertent as it was, which bed Xelie liked.

It was the stinky bed. The bed that carried the scent of all the other dogs, the friends that she loved, the friends that she cared for. That's what had been missing from the new fancy beds I had gotten her. Yes they were beautiful, and luxuriously comfortable, but they lacked the most important thing, they lacked the smell of love that Xelie and her fabulous nose detected.

Xelie, Nell and I spent quite a long time on the porch that evening just reveling in the moment, in being together, in loving each other and appreciating each second as it came and went.

43.

Independence day

It was Friday, July 4th, 2014, Independence Day. When I awoke, Xelie was still with me, Nell curled up nearby. Xelie was very very weak. I gently picked her up and took her outside. Somehow, amazingly, she was able to stand just long enough to potty.

I brought her back in and set her down on blankets I had spread out on the living room floor. She was still alert and her eyes still unbelievably bright. I set a bowl of water down in front of her. She drank. I then offered a little food. As promised, she ate several mouthfuls, just enough to take her pill.

I told her to stay put, that I'd be back. I didn't want her to attempt to stand and then hurt herself falling. After letting the housedogs out of the upstairs bedroom, I followed them outside to begin morning chores.

Being a holiday, I had scheduled a number of lessons for the day in the weeks prior. I had been conflicted about whether or not to cancel given Xelie's condition. Her body could barely sustain her and her gums were now extremely pale. I thought, perhaps, my constant presence was making it impossible for her to let go.

So as difficult as it was, I left my beloved Xelie inside as I went out to give lessons. I checked on her in between each run of each and every dog, to make sure she was comfortable and that she had water, or anything else she might need.

At some point, mid-morning while I had been outside, Xelie had managed to move from the living room into the breakfast nook. I found her sleeping peacefully at the base of the stairs, just below the window that looked out over the back pasture that'd we'd enjoyed so much the night before.

I don't know if she had wanted to look out the window at the dogs working below, or if she'd been contemplating how to get to the bedroom and her dog friends upstairs. Whatever the case, she looked comfortable. If this was the place she wanted to lie, then by God this was the place she would stay.

I believe it was on my way either to or from the living room to retrieve Xelie's bowl of water, that I noticed... Two beautiful locks of Xelie's wavy golden hair. This was the very beginning of a mysterious theme of two.

It's simply dog hair, what's the big deal you might ask? With as many dogs as traipsed in and out the house, hair was certainly not a novelty. But this wasn't just hair that had been shed and floated across the tile. These were neat, tidy locks, as if someone had cut them just for me.

Now she's gone over the edge, you're probably thinking. Perhaps yes, perhaps no. It has always been my custom when I've lost an animal dear to me, to save a beautiful lock of their hair as a memento of our love. I had always taken it after their spirit had passed.

That morning, finding those two distinct, exquisite locks, there was no doubt in my mind, I wouldn't have to take a memento from Xelie, she had already given me one as a gift.

How did she know? Was it her, or was a greater power at work? I didn't much consider the option that it could have been a coincidence. In any event, I quietly picked up those yellow locks of hair, and respectfully set them in a safe place upstairs.

Xelie was sleeping, each breath, deep and deliberate, as I silently slipped back outside.

The holiday had allowed three of my Saturday regulars to come this Friday as well. Laura, Joy and Nancy had become good friends and I always looked forward to visiting and working with them.

They had grown to love Xelie and asked how she was. I told them… Through the tears, I told them I thought today would be the day… I couldn't continue, they didn't need me to…

It wasn't long after that I again checked on Xelie. I bent down beside her, rested my hand on her shoulder. No response, she didn't stir even the slightest bit. She's leaving, I thought.

And then, in spite of myself, and my desire to allow her simply to let go, I panicked and called out, "Xelie!" Her eyes fluttered open, her spirit clearly returning from some distant place.

Why had I done that? Looking back, no matter how much I wanted to set her free, I couldn't let her go. She looked at me. I can't remember if she rose from her side to an upright lying position.

I only remember that I had called her back. Back to me. Back to this life. Back to the breakfast nook at the foot of the stairs that led to the bedroom where she and Nell and her other pack friends had spent so many years together.

After a short time, she lay back over on her side and closed her eyes once again. I returned back outside.

I was trying to lose myself in my work, I have no doubt of it now. I was trying to distract from the pain of our impending separation.

As I headed back into the upper field, I thought I was doing pretty well. I knew this day would come, I'd known it for weeks. And effectively denied it for a lifetime, if I'm honest. I had remained strong for Xelie and would continue to do so, assisting in any way I could.

Laura was up with her little sheltie, Rita. Rita had been coming on like gangbusters in the past number of months and her enthusiasm had been a delight.

But on this morning, when Laura sent her to gather, Rita wouldn't run, at least not the way she had every other weekend. The joy and speed she had come to display were gone, uncertainty and apprehension had taken their place. After a number of attempts we simply stopped; Rita just wasn't herself.

Or perhaps it wasn't Rita at all, at the root of the problem. Dogs are intuitive, and with all that was happening on that 4th day of July, perhaps Rita was saying she couldn't work -- and neither should I.

As we walked out of the field, I suggested Laura have a conversation with Rita and inquire what the issue might be. Laura agreed and off to the dog pool they went for a cool off and a chat.

Nancy had been inside. She remarked about Xelie's breathing, so slow and so deep. I went back in the house; Xelie was in the same place she'd been when I called her back to this life. Her breathing was the same as it had been since the morning when we awoke.

Before I headed down into the large pasture beneath the window where Xelie lay, I asked Laura if she would mind taking a look at her. You see, Laura was in the medical profession and dealt with cancer patients day in and day out. If anyone would know how close Xelie was to leaving us all, Laura would.

I asked her to come get me if she thought the end was near. Laura agreed, heading toward the house as Joy and I made our way down the hill into the field. Images of Xelie delighting in her sheep flashed in my mind's eye as we passed by the places where Xelie and I had worked.

I wasn't long into Joy's lesson when Laura emerged from the house and started in our direction. Oh no, I thought...

"You should be with Xelie", Laura said. She couldn't tell me how long, but her certainty was clear. Joy nodded her agreement, "Don't worry about us". I told them to help themselves to sheep for as long as they liked and then started up the hill, silent tears streaming down my cheeks.

By the time I reached Xelie I had pulled myself together. I couldn't expect she'd feel free to move on if I was sobbing like a baby.

I sat on the floor beside her, gently stroking that beautiful head, those unique tufted ears. My hand ran across her body, the body that once upon time, not so very long ago, had been powerful and athletic. That body that had taken her on so many adventures. That body that had moved those many sheep with confidence and grace. That body that had helped her govern her pack with inspired wisdom and love.

And now that body was failing... As I lay on the floor beside her, it was clear... It was Xelie's will alone keeping her alive. I went to the porch and grabbed her favorite stinky bed, laid a potty pad across it and then lifted her atop it.

It was clear she was having a terribly hard time letting go. She wanted to stay. I wanted her to stay. We wanted to stay together. But lying on the floor that afternoon on the 4th of July, neither of us had a choice.

Whether we liked it or not, it was indeed Independence Day, for both Xelie and for me.

44.

Not yet

I explained to Xelie that when two spirits love each other the way we loved each other, they always stay connected. The options are endless -- in another life, again in this life, on the other side...

I reassured her that her friends were already there, in the new place she was going, and that they were waiting for her. There was my newfie Dot, and Annie her young friend with whom she had so enjoyed exploring, and I imagined that her mother might be there as well. I remembered Lucy, but didn't know that Xelie would take comfort in that thought, so I left her off the list.

I told her they were waiting and would be happy to show her

around. She wasn't going to be alone, that was for sure.

I added, that in her new place, she could be in charge, and be alpha, as she'd been in charge here, if she so wished. Although I didn't know for sure, I suspected that this was true, because in heaven, one can do whatever makes one happy. They've earned the right, right?

I had been in text contact with Laura, keeping her abreast of the situation. She asked whether there were any dogs to whom Xelie needed to say goodbye?

Good thought. I began letting them out of the bedroom, one by one. Nell was first. She visited with Xelie and I knew that she knew, but wasn't the least bit upset. Then my top male, Mosse, alpha behind Xelie. He gave her kisses, ignoring the dog treats on the floor in front of her. Treats he would have devoured on any other occasion. Cora had nothing to say, (ungrateful bitch), she just tried to snarf food from the counter top. And Molly, was just Molly, bullying the others as she always did.

After I'd let them all outside, Xelie happily ate four pepperoni slices and drank quite a bit of water. I wrote Laura, "The sparkle in her eyes could blind you to the fact she's sick".

And that was the way of Xelie, a sparkling spirit, casting light on all who came in contact with her. Even now at the brink of death, she was an example of everything good and pure. She didn't feel sorry for herself, or give way to the pain, if she felt any discomfort; her eyes remained bright, positive, loving and strong.

It was at that point that I laid my head on the stinky bed beside her and closed my eyes. I emptied my mind as best I could. I will help her let go, that will be my gift, I will escort her to the freedom of her new spirit life.

When my friend Carla had passed more than ten years before, I had assisted her in this same manner. For hours and hours I had meditated, hand gently upon her, doing my best to be helpful, doing my best to help her let go. Like Xelie, Carla wanted to stay and she clung to each breath with a desperate hunger for life.

178

I remember the knowing, the knowing I felt, that there was someone Carla needed to see, someone to whom she desperately wanted to say goodbye. There was something Carla had left undone or unsaid.

It had been a long hard struggle, but finally Carla's body just wouldn't sustain her spirit, no matter how hard she fought to stay.

That journey with Carla had been an inspirational experience. It left me with an incredible peace and with absolutely no doubt in my mind that our spirits continue well beyond our faded bodies.

My eyes were closed, my mind was quiet as Xelie and I began the journey. We moved from the darkness to the edge of a luxurious pasture. Mountains cut majestically into the background sky as the sun rested low atop the peaks, casting a warm inviting glow over the stunning surround.

It was a happy place with a playful sense of whimsy. Xelie stood beside me, tall, curious. She gazed over this new pasture as she had gazed, the night before, over our field from her vantage point atop the stinky bed on the porch at the top the hill.

In this new place, at this moment, she gazed at her lush green future, a future unknown. Last evening she had gazed over her past, past minutes, and days and years she had so happily spent there.

At least that's the way I saw it, Xelie of course had been in the moment, at least that's what I presume.

We stood at the edge of this marvelous place for only several seconds all told, when suddenly Xelie turned and looked at me. Panic is not exactly the right word, but her communication was clear – "not yet!"

She rolled to an upright position, abruptly ending our journey. There was something or someone holding her here. Was it Sue? Sue had promised Xelie the day before, that she would be by again today.

A huge storm was rolling in, and unlike the day before, this time it wasn't going to miss us. That day it rained at my home in Texas, in July. In all the time I have lived here since 2005, I can hardly remember rain in July or June even. I can hardly remember it raining much past the beginning of

May. Maybe once, in 2007 it rained in the summer… Suffice to say, it's very rare.

So here on the day that would probably be Xelie's last, a huge storm heralded the event, just as the violent storm had heralded the beginning of the end on the day Xelie was diagnosed with lymphoma. Tempests distinctly marked the beginning and the end of our very special time together, Xelie's and mine.

In any event, the meteorological event brought rain and cooler temperatures yet again. And when it had cleared, I let all the dogs out.

Maybe Xelie simply wants one more evening out with the pack. I had denied her this privilege the night before following her fall. Perhaps she had intended to say her goodbyes at that time when I whisked her back in the house.

This time, I carried Xelie out and placed her down on a comfortable spot of sand near the back door. Nell stayed nearby as was always her custom. A light rain sprinkled down upon us, and being in the moment, we all enjoyed it.

The dogs played with each other and visited Xelie from time to time. It wasn't long before Sue arrived. She pulled up a chair beside Xelie and me, and just as we had the day before, we stroked her as we spoke.

I don't remember how long we remained like this; all I can tell you is it was peaceful. Xelie was happy; I sensed this was what she wanted, to be surrounded by everyone she loved.

But there was one more thing. As Sue and I sat talking to Xelie and each other, I noticed Xelie, more than once, lift her head and gaze toward the dog pool. She wants a nice soak, I thought.

Sue kept watch over Xelie as I put the other dogs up. She was now fragile and I wanted to avoid any inadvertent accidents. I wanted to make certain her ending would be peaceful and glorious. I wanted to make certain her ending was all that she wanted it to be.

I rinsed out the pool, refilling it with cool fresh water. I lifted Xelie and placed her gently in the water. She melted into the pleasure of it, closing her eyes, soaking, soaking up the feeling for one last time. She had always loved the pool and a dip in the water. From the time she'd been young.

It was the first time ever, in Xelie's adult life, that her hind end and tail didn't rest on the rim and drape outside the water. On this evening, her last dip in the pool, she curled her entire body into the water and relished the sensation.

Her strength almost gone, I supported her head, preventing it from dropping too deeply below the surface. I held her head in my hands, knowing we'd reached the end of her list. The end of the final things she needed to do.

It wouldn't have surprised me if she'd passed then and there – but she didn't...

45.

The final journey

After a time, I lifted her out of the water and laid her on a fresh towel. And with another, I lovingly dried her as best I could. She was going back in the AC and I didn't want her to be cold.

And when she was dry, I carried her in my arms back into the living room. I found it surprising, both then and now, that Xelie didn't seem to mind in the slightest that I was transferring her from place to place. There was absolutely no resistance whatsoever. No humiliation.

It was as if she knew, knew all this was playing out exactly as it should. While she was helping me, she was allowing me to help her. Life is, after all, give and take, is it not? Perhaps this was what she was trying to tell me, at least one of the things...

As was her wish, I placed her on the stinky bed that I'd moved into the living room atop the many blankets that were spread there. Sue was getting ready to leave. "I'll see you to..." I cut her off. Not the word tomorrow. "Don't say that" I said. "She'll wait". Sue nodded and said her final goodbye.

Now it was time. I turned off the lights and stretched out on the floor beside Xelie, my hand on her left front leg. I closed my eyes and emptied my mind. Now we'll journey, to that beautiful meadow; that whimsical pasture in the mountains where we'd journeyed before.

It was then, as Xelie and I lay on the floor together, preparing for the final journey, that Nell began to circle us. Over and over, she moved around us, orbiting, circumnavigating some mysterious energy bubble.

Perhaps it was her way of "herding" Xelie to her final passage. She traveled only to her left, on the "go-bye". Awfully close to "Good bye"...

In any event, to this day, I do not know Nell's exact purpose. But Nell did. And I imagine Xelie did. And in the end, that's what mattered.

After a time, Nell settled to the floor nearby. Xelie and I remained, touching, on the floor together for quite some time. And then, she pulled her leg back, away from me. After a moment, I rested my hand on her again. It wasn't long and she pulled it back again.

My touch is making it impossible; that was the message I received. I withdrew my arm and waited there for quite some time, still meditating, still trying to help her let go.

The music was playing, new age, ethereal. It was a satellite station and I always had it on. Xelie had listened to it down in the living room when she'd had the run of the house. She'd listened to it for almost four weeks.

There was one song in particular; it played as we journeyed to that lush green mountain pasture, the place that to me was certainly the "other side". It too was whimsical, the melody light and full of hope. It was to this song, I could imagine Xelie, in this wonderful new place, with a body strong and whole, frolicking, running and free once again. This was Xelie's song...

As I lay beside Xelie, no longer physically connected by touch, the music continued to play. Not Xelie's song, but other music, soothing, almost unearthly.

The music, maybe it's the music holding her here, I thought. I reached for the remote and turned it off. Not long after, I drifted off to sleep. Sometime an hour or two later, I was awakened by a smell; Xelie had an accident. I cleaned it up and spread a new potty pad on the stinky bed and placed her back on top. She was limp, barely conscious. Her body was finally shutting down.

At some point, not long after that, her breathing changed. Even slower, deeper. She'll be gone by sunrise, I was certain of it.

She was not. When I awakened, she was still breathing, still slow, still deep. Her head was faced away from me in the dimly lit room; somehow she'd managed to get her head off the bed and the blankets and onto the cool tile.

I wanted to touch her, talk to her, but I was afraid I'd bring her back. I slipped quietly from the room and began my morning routine. When all the dogs were fed and turned out to play, I returned inside.

Xelie was still breathing. I'll spend my breakfast with her for one final time. I moved into the living room and over to Xelie, to that gorgeous wheaten head...

And wanted to die myself. Her eyes were wide open. She was conscious as conscious could be, and she couldn't move. I was horrified. All this time, since the time her breathing had changed, I had assumed she was unconscious and almost gone.

But here she was, not at all peaceful. Quite disturbed in fact, by the fact she couldn't move, she couldn't – anything... But just lay there, prisoner to her failing body.

"I'm so sorry. I'm so sorry. I'm going to help". It was six in the morning when I phoned the mobile vet. He was sound asleep but, thankfully, answered the phone. He agreed to come but it would be at least an hour.

And for that hour I sat with Xelie, stroking her, telling her she would soon be free. Telling her how much she meant me, and what an amazing friend she had been.

I explained again how we could be together in the next life or on the other side, or in this life in another body. And then it finally occurred to me to say that she could come back whenever she wanted, with or without a body. We'd all love to see her.

Why was she holding on, even now? It was absolutely unbelievable.

From where I sit here today, I think I understand. As I mentioned earlier, from the time Xelie was diagnosed, every morning and every evening, and many times in between, I'd break down crying and say, "I don't want her to go. I don't want her to go".

I must have repeated that phrase a hundred times or more. Never when Xelie was with me, always when I was alone, when Xelie was either outside or out of range. You see, I didn't want to upset her; I didn't want her to see me so sad.

But dogs are intuitive and many times psychic. I thought I'd been so clever acting as if all was okay with her passing on. Intellectually it was the truth, but emotionally it was a big fat stinking lie. Not an intentional one…

Xelie was holding on for me. Now I'm almost certain. And as the universe would have it, if it was me keeping her here, it was up to me to help her go.

A text rang out on my phone; the vet was on his way. It wouldn't be long now. I told Xelie help was on its way and I'd be right back. Quickly, I put up the dogs and unlocked the gate.

185

When I returned, she was still breathing, in the same spot I left her. I sat with her on the floor cradling her head in my arms, sending all the love I had in my heart, in my life, sending it to Xelie, my beloved Xelie.

The dogs in the kennel began to bark. The vet had arrived. I gently rested Xelie's head on the floor and went to greet him. I went back into the house, back to Xelie. Together, we waited for her ending to enter.

Blood was barely moving through Xelie's veins as he administered the first shot, to simply allow her to drift unconscious into sleep. It wasn't working. He explained that sometimes, when they're this compromised, the drugs don't work the way you'd like.

My text started sounding off, over and over from my phone in the kitchen. Obviously I didn't answer.

The vet couldn't get a vein, the first one had collapsed. I cradled Xelie; "it's okay, you'll feel better soon." Finally, he was successful and slipped the needle in her arm. I gazed into Xelie's eyes with all the comfort and love I possessed, as he pressed down the plunger.

Xelie's eyes began to close and before the last bit of liquid disappeared from the syringe, I felt Xelie leave her body. She was finally free. Free to move on. Free to frolic in that beautiful place she and I had discovered together.

But being Xelie, she embraced her new freedom with some ideas of her own. The moment she left her body, all the dogs in the bedroom just above us began to stir and move excitedly about.

I smiled. "She visiting her friends" I exclaimed. I knew it without a doubt, she was in my upstairs bedroom, the room that had been her home, saying her final farewell to Nell, Molly and Cora.

Xelie's end was finally here.

Or was it?

photo by Bob Degus

46.

Xelie's last voyage

Xelie relinquished her body on July 5th , 2014, several minutes past 7:45. If I had to guess, I would say it was 7:48 am. Sue had texted just after we had administered the first drug, the drug to make her sleep.

"Checking in with you. How are things?" That's what she'd written at 7:45 am. She again connected, for the third time in two weeks, to the moment of a loved one's parting.

The process of helping Xelie let go had begun to be sure, but there had been complications. The sleeping drug hadn't worked. Then Xelie's vein had collapsed. It had taken a bit to find another vein strong enough to carry her ending.

I believe Xelie passed at 7:48 am.

I spread a blanket over a tarp in the trunk of the Honda. The vet emerged, Xelie's body in his arms. He carefully placed her on the blanket and began to close the lid. I stopped him and covered Xelie, all but her scruffy wheaten head.

I paid the vet for his service. He had been kind and sympathetic and wonderful with Xelie. I was so very grateful he had come, as he drove away that morning.

It wasn't more than a minute or two when Laura and Joy pulled to a stop in the driveway a short distance from the car and the trunk where Xelie lay. They emerged, mortified... Death is always easier when you don't have to look at it face to face.

I explained to them what had happened and how I had found Xelie conscious when I thought all that remained was her body shutting down. And when the explanation was complete, I sorted a group of sheep and invited them to work.

It was Saturday morning and I was unsure whether or not my local vet was open. You see almost a year prior, when Lucy had passed away, I had taken her body there so they could handle her cremation.

I had already made arrangements for Xelie with the specialty clinic more than an hour away. They were open 24 hours and since it was a holiday weekend and I didn't know when she would pass, it gave me peace of mind to know I had an arrangement

But I preferred the local clinic. They had done a beautiful job with Lucy, returning her remains in a beautiful wooden box, granting her all the love and respect that her life had deserved. Thankfully, they were open that Saturday morning.

But before I went anywhere I needed a shower. You see, I had wanted to spend every moment I could with Xelie and I hadn't wanted her to be alone. At least not until I thought my presence was a detriment. And even then, separating from her had been difficult.

In any event, I hadn't showered since the morning of the 4th and I was filthy, covered in dirt and sand and other things to remain unmentioned.

As the water rinsed the past twenty-four hours from my body, I realized just how tired I was. I hadn't slept much in the past number of weeks, and in spite of the countless joyous and amazing moments Xelie and I had shared, the pain and prior knowledge of our final separation had been utterly draining.

I would take Xelie on her final voyage, and then I would sleep...

47.

No, not Nell...

I put on a fresh set of clothes and stepped out of the bathroom just in time to see Nell, staggering, hardly able to remain on her feet. She was in the bedroom, my bedroom, the room Xelie's spirit had visited less than thirty minutes before.

"Oh no, not Nell. Not her too". I had been worried about Nell and how she would respond to Xelie's departure. They had been so close. And now here she was, barely able to stand.

I had planned to bring Nell with me on Xelie's final car ride. It was only suiting that she and I, the two most important people in Xelie's life, see to it that her body was delivered into respectful, caring hands.

But now there was absolutely no doubt. Nell was coming with me, not just for Xelie, but to have a doctor look her over. I whisked Nell up in my arms just as I had done with Xelie for the past several days. I carried her down the stairs and out the back door.

As we emerged from the house, Laura caught sight of us and approached. I set Nell down, feet first. She was unsteady, but she could stand. As I was explaining to Laura what had just transpired, Nell moved to the Honda and sniffed at the trunk where Xelie's body laid.

Allowing Nell a moment with her friend who had just passed, I then put her in the backseat and headed to the house to retrieve the keys. Laura called out "She just wants to go. She nodded just now when I asked her".

She nodded. I stopped dead in my tracks.

I hadn't told Laura that in the past number of weeks, Xelie had begun to nod at me. It was a gesture characteristic to my long passed Newfoundland, Dot, who used to look at me and nod on a very regular basis. And since Xelie's diagnosis, she had adopted the habit. I had just assumed that Dot was around assisting Xelie in the process.

I had explained to Xelie that if she chose to return, she needed to give me a sign, an unmistakable sign, so that I would know it was her. The only two dogs I have ever known to nod, were first Dot and then Xelie.

And now Nell? Nell was nodding?

As I drove to the clinic, I kept thinking, suspecting it was Xelie's way of saying farewell. As I said, in the past upon losing an animal close to me, they had all returned for one final farewell with a signature behavior or sign that couldn't be ignored.

And sometimes, they used another dog close to them to assist. Dot had done this when she passed away. Sprocket, my other Newfie, had allowed her the use of his body for a final farewell.

You see, each evening before bed, I would let Dot and Sprocket out to potty. Sprocket with all his physical ailments, would simply step off the back porch and relieve himself right there on the grass.

But Dot, she would always make her way out the picket fence gate, across the gravel driveway, to the storage shed, where she'd search for the perfect spot underneath a giant pine tree.

On the evening of the day of Dot's death, when I let Sprocket out alone for his nightly potty, he didn't stop at the foot of the porch as he always did. Instead he made his way, following Dot's usual path, out to the storage shed where he relieved himself under the pine.

And when he returned he stopped in the open picket fence gate and stared at me. "Hello Dot" I had said; I knew it was her. And here she was for one last visit, to say good bye and to let me know everything was all right.

And I've told you about Annie, and how Carla came to her rescue and mine.

And poor Sprocket, who passed away, spending the evening in a veterinary clinic alone. I had left him only because my vet had reassured me he'd be fine.

You see my husband and I loved candles. And each evening, we'd fire up tea lights that rested inside matching amber glass holders set on the mantle of our fireplace. On this evening, something happened that had never happened before and has never happened since.

My husband and I were visiting, as we did at the end of each day, when one of the mantle tea lights began to hiss, then roared quietly into a cylinder of fire that projected well above the top of the candleholder. Sprocket entered my mind. "Oh no, I don't like this", I had said to my husband.

The following morning we were informed that Sprocket had passed away that evening before, the evening the candle had plumed into a column of fire.

And then there was my horse, Paula. And of course Carla, a very strong spirit, who made symbolic appearances not only to me, but to many others, especially those of us who had spent the last three days of her life helping with her transition.

Now you may be thinking to yourself, this lady's nuts. And everyone's entitled to their own opinion. But I can assure you, I'm not.

I don't hear voices and I do not hallucinate. But I do pay attention. I pay attention, when things are unusual or atypical, or utterly typical but completely out of context.

Or to be accurate I should say, I used to listen until the lost years when I forgot. When I forgot what a wonderful mysterious universe surrounds us. When I got bogged down and caught up in the material minutiae of day-to-day life. And now, thanks to Xelie, I was paying attention again.

Nell had never nodded before, not until that morning in the back of the Honda on the heels of Xelie's passing. It couldn't have been my imagination, because I didn't see it; Nell had nodded to Laura. And Laura didn't know a thing about the recent nodding. It was a sign from Xelie, I strongly suspected.

It was now closing in on 9am. As I drove, I placed a call to the clinic, to make an appointment for Nell. Ten o'clock was the earliest time anyone could look at her. I told them I'd take it.

We arrived at the clinic and pulled around the back. This was where they received animals that had recently passed away. The two vet techs lifted Xelie from the trunk and carried her inside. I followed. They asked if I'd like an imprint of her paw. "Yes, front right", I'd replied without giving it a second thought. It was her strongest leg, the one that caused her no pain.

I stepped out the back door, clinging to a small box, her paw print inside. It was all I had left of Xelie's physical existence. I started toward the car and saw Nell staring at me, and then the clinic door, and then me. Her message was clear, she wanted to say good bye to Xelie.

I stopped the techs just before the door closed; they were kind enough to let me bring Nell inside for a last visit.

Holding Nell in my arms, I stopped just in front of Xelie's body. She looked. And then so did I... The body I had left only a minute or two before, now seemed different. There was an energy... She almost looked alive. I placed my hand on her side; she was warm.

"Some of them stay warm longer than others", I was informed. I can't remember if it was my expression alone or if I actually said something, but the vet tech drew up her stethoscope and placed it on Xelie's heart. After a moment, "She's gone".

photo by Bob Degus

48.

A revelation

Nell and I pulled the Honda back around the front of the clinic and parked. We'd have to wait a bit for Nell's appointment.

I lifted her from the back seat and placed her on the ground. No wobble. She was stable. She sniffed the grass as if nothing was wrong, then walked into the clinic without a symptom in the world.

We took a seat in the waiting room. A man and his child were seated across from us accompanying an elderly dog that was also waiting to be seen. I asked the dog's age. Fourteen, they responded.

Uncharacteristically, Nell was quite curious about the elder canine across from her, pulling toward him, sniffing. And then two cattle dogs entered. She wagged and tugged at the leash, trying to get closer, just as a young pup might do.

This was altogether bizarre. Nell had always been aloof of nature. The only dogs she'd ever sought out were Xelie and her own pups. I'd never seen her be so outgoing, ever.

They called to the man and the older dog; it was time for their appointment. As they headed toward the exam rooms I saw the reason the dog was here. A large tumor hung from his side. Cancer, I thought. I turned back to Nell, sniffing about curiously, trying to be social. There appeared to be absolutely nothing wrong with her.

And then it occurred to me... Maybe this isn't Nell; maybe this is Xelie. Crazy I know, but all these behaviors, they belonged to outgoing Xelie, not conservative Nell. And Nell's miraculous recovery, from wobbly instability to stable normalcy. I almost laughed out loud as the thoughts raced through my mind.

Could Nell have become unstable when Xelie entered her body? Nell was old after all, and somewhat fragile this past year. Could Xelie have recreated the form she had just relinquished, one of physical weakness, inability to walk with the need of being carried?

Had both Xelie and Nell conspired to make certain Nell would join me on Xelie's final car ride? Had Xelie used Nell as a vessel to get back to her body in an effort to re-enter her lifeless form? Had that been the sign of life I'd seen, in the back, in the morgue? Had Xelie's spirit been trying it's damnedest to re-enter her lifeless body?

Had Xelie tried to tell me in the waiting room that it had been her, not Nell, when she sniffed at the older dog with cancer? When she was friendly and outgoing with the cattle dogs that entered?

All these thoughts... And which, if any of them, or all of them, were true?

In any event, Nell seemed fine. And sensing that her symptoms had simply been a visitation from Xelie, I went to the front desk and cancelled her appointment. The staff member was shocked and inquired if I was certain I wanted to do that?

I looked at Nell, and I knew. Xelie's paw prints were all over the events of the past sixty minutes. She'd even made certain to give me a literal paw print, just in case I was so thick I couldn't figure it out. After all, I had not been offered that service when I had dropped Lucy there the year before.

I was sure. I reached for a checkbook to pay for Xelie's arrangements. It was my mother's checkbook from an account she rarely used. She had insisted on paying for Xelie's cremation and I had accepted her generous gift.

As I flipped through the carbons to get to a fresh check, I came across the payment we had made for Lucy's cremation the summer before. The date caught my eye. Lucy passed away on 8-5-2013. Xelie passed away on 7-5-2014. Exactly eleven months to the day.

I'm almost afraid to write this part for fear you'll stop reading. You see, if you add up the number of each departure date, Xelie's and Lucy's, each one equals the number ten. (8+5+2+1+3= 19 – 9+1=10) The time of Xelie's exact passing also added up to the number ten. I discovered Xelie's first lump on a Saturday, and exactly 28 days later, Xelie died. Add two and eight and you get the number ten. And finally, it had been ten years since I had sat down to write a book, a script, or anything other than an e-mail and a text. And the date the document that is this book, this tribute to Xelie, was created is listed as 7-7-14. The number ten.

I have no idea what the number ten means or meant in the scheme of these events. It is simply an observation of yet another thing, a very unusual coincidence, of something that was certainly not the norm.

Everything happens for a reason, that's what I believe. Perhaps the number ten is simply to illustrate a connection, to make plain that none of these events were an accident. To affirm that things were as they should be. Or perhaps it's something else, or something more that I've not yet come to realize. You don't know what you don't know, right?

Tate

photo by Bob Degus

49.

Having a field day

I drove home feeling uplifted. I know it sounds bizarre, on the heels of Xelie's death. But I was so intrigued and impressed with Xelie's ability to reach across the barrier between the spirit plane and the physical realm that all I felt at the moment was awe. I didn't yet feel the grief of loss, because she was still here.

When I got home, I parked in the usual spot. Nell jumped out of the car and she and I headed toward the kennels. Joy and Laura were astounded at Nell's miraculous recovery and probably a bit shocked at the smile on my face.

I began to relay the events of the clinic, when Joy's new dog, Tate, trotted happily up to me. He had not done this since Joy bought him.

You see, Tate had been my dog and I loved him very much. He's the only dog I've ever known with a sense of humor. He had been an outstanding stock dog, winning trial after trial and qualifying for the finals every year he was eligible. Except for the last when he moved into Open...

It had been clear when I first got Tate and had begun to train him, that there was something amiss with his eyes; he simply did not see properly and it was more than farsightedness or nearsightedness. In 2009 he was diagnosed with CEA, Collie Eye Anomaly. His eyes were definitely compromised.

Texas Sheepdog Association rules mandate that when a dog reaches a certain number of points in their class, they must progress to the next level into the next most difficult class. With Tate's talent and consistency, he had pointed out quickly and by the beginning of 2009, had been required to move into the most advanced level, the Open class.

Beginning competition in the Open was the beginning of the end of Tate's career. The gathers were over too great a distance and he simply couldn't see the sheep. In addition, Tate had suffered additional loss to his sight that had also made him very anxious. It was this combination that lead to his permanent retirement on the trial field with me as his handler.

He had worked with me as a lesson helper, off and on over the years, but mostly he lay in my bedroom during the day with Xelie, Nell, Molly and Cora. Not at all what Tate wanted. Or me either, for that matter.

As much as I dearly loved Tate and his very special companionship, I always felt a little guilty that he wasn't working much at all any longer. He was one of the keenest dogs I have ever had; he lived to work. Retirement seemed so unfair.

A number of months earlier, I'd had an idea, a possible way for Tate to work. Laura was headed off to Minnesota on vacation and she was going to attend two dog trials while there. Laura had only one dog for a border collie trial, a long way to go for one dog. So I offered Tate as a second dog to run. Just because I couldn't run him, didn't mean someone else couldn't run him, someone who wasn't an Open handler, that is.

Excited by the prospect, Laura began to practice with Tate. And Tate was ecstatic to be working again. Save the details, but at one point, Joy gave Tate a spin, and from that point forward they began to fall in love.

I offered another dog to Laura, a dog ultimately more suited to her, and Joy began to run Tate regularly.

Long story short, one thing lead to another. Tate loved Joy and was happy to work. And Joy wanted to make their new relationship official. From that point forward, Tate would hardly look at me. I sensed he was afraid that I was going to take him back, back to a life of retirement.

Only a week or two prior to that morning of July 5th, I had reassured Tate that he could stay with Joy for as long as he wanted. He smiled, looking at me again for the first time. But just because he looked at me, didn't mean he approached me to work with him. He and Joy were now bonded, it was very clear.

So when Tate came running up to me that morning as I stood in the driveway talking to Laura and Joy, we all three were quite surprised. He started toward the small training pen, then stopped and looked back at me as if to say "C'mon, lets go work!"

Tate trotted past Mosse's kennel. On any other morning or afternoon or evening, Mosse would have lunged at the chain link, snarling at Tate. The two dogs hated each other. But on this morning, Tate trotted by and Mosse just lay there quiet and relaxed.

We all exchanged a look; this is too weird. Tate stopped and looked at me again, beckoning me to join him. And all three of us knew, this was not Tate.

As Xelie had become weaker, I had taken to letting her work sheep much more in the upper areas of my property so as to avoid the hill, climbing up and down. She and I had moved sheep in and out of this small training pen over and over just the week before.

Tate had not worked in that small pen for months, maybe even longer. And there was a set of sheep loose out in the open nearby. But ignoring the available set, Tate trotted to the small training pen, waiting, waiting for me to join him.

I can't remember which of us said it. "Xelie?" Joy nodded for me to go ahead and work him. So into the little pen Tate and I went. He was usually quite zippy and fast, but today he was relaxed and graceful.

He didn't squeeze the sheep bubble like he so often loved to do, he just moved around them, respecting their space, balancing the group to me. I could almost hear Xelie saying "Whoa, so this is what a border collie body feels like. It's so agile and fast." And I wanted to add, and pain free…

She was having the time of her life running in Tate's body. Or was it the time of her death? In any event, just as Sprocket had done for Dot, Tate had given Xelie his body on loan and Xelie was delighted. And when we were finished, I said, "Okay, Xelie, let's go". And the dog usually named Tate came trotting over to me, beaming.

I opened the gate and out he went, dashing happily across the grass. And then his countenance shifted and he changed. I suppose it was as Xelie left and Tate returned. And from that point forward, Tate never looked back and returned to Joy.

Joy, Laura and I stared at each other in utter amazement. I was happy that they had seen the same thing I had seen. That they had drawn the same conclusion I had drawn.

Because when things like this happen, and it's very rare that they do, one can't help but question whether one's imagination has become a little overactive.

But on this day, looking at Laura and Joy, I knew I had seen what I thought I had seen, and felt what I thought I had felt, from the moment Xelie left her body until this moment right now.

photo by Bob Degus

50.

The arteeest

I stepped into the house after lessons, exhausted, ready for a nap. I gazed over the living room; it was exactly as I had left it, exactly as it had been when Xelie breathed her last breath. I stared at it a minute, at the stinky bed, now empty.

Images of Xelie, and all that had transpired over the past twenty-four hours, flashed through my mind. And when I felt ready, I moved to Xelie's favorite bed, picked it up, and returned it to its place on the screened-in porch.

It was time to return the living room to its original condition. And when all the blankets and accessories had been removed, I settled onto the couch for some much needed rest.

But as sheer exhaustion sometimes has it, I was too tired to sleep. I closed my eyes anyway and began to meditate. Before long, Xelie danced in my imagination. Her "other side" theme song began to play over the TV.

As the whimsical melody floated through the air, Xelie was bounding, free and light in my mind. Alive and happy, she ran... Racing over the sand... The sand? There was no sand in that lush mountain pasture. But there was in... My back pasture?!

I bolted upright and went to the window overlooking the field. In almost the same spot Xelie had been that last evening on the porch when she and Nell gazed out over their kingdom.

I looked and scanned the field, moving from the sandy area to the oasis, the place under two stately trees where dogs went, including Xelie, to cool off in water filled kiddie pools. And there she was, Xelie, laying comfortably in the shade staring up at the house.

I blinked; she was still there. My heart started pounding. I couldn't believe it. I just could not believe my eyes. And then I realized I didn't have on my glasses.

I quickly snatched them up and went back to the window. And looked back at the spot. With things a little more in focus I could see it was a goat weed, actually several, but the arrangement of one in particular was shaped identically to Xelie's head and those oh so unique tufted ears.

I squinted, and even with my glasses on, it was Xelie again. I opened my eyes to a normal position, it was a group of weeds.

To believe or not believe? To make the leap? To open up to just a smidgen of the mystery our universe has to offer?

I choose to believe. I believe it was a plant and I believe it was also Xelie. How creative Xelie was, what an arteeeest.

And what an incredibly strong, intelligent spirit she was. She had been with me all day, leaving clue after clue, serving both her needs and mine. Which is how it should be in a perfect world. It was a win, win…

She had given me so very much in her life and in the last four weeks. And now, here she was bestowing yet more food for thought. As I mentioned earlier, in the past many of my loved animal companions had returned for one final farewell. But Xelie, I'd need a calculator to count up all the clues she'd left from 7:48 am until now.

And Xelie knew, that I knew. And she was as happy as I. Yes, things were different, but she and I were still together, just as I had promised and probably as she had already known.

That night, out with the pack, the very first night without physical Xelie present, I had to say thank you, although those words were hardly enough. Even though we couldn't see her wonderful scruffy body any longer, she was still alpha of the pack. She was still looking out for all of us, with genuine, everlasting, caring and love.

51.

One more run

Sunday came; it was the first dawn without Xelie. As I let the dogs out onto the screened in porch, Mosse stopped at the stinky bed, giving it a good long once over with his nose.

I opened the back door to the yard and they all bounded out – so strange not to see Xelie, her wheaten yellow color in stark contrast to the black and white border collies; strange not to see her trotting happily into a new day with her distinctive bobbing gate and awesome tufted ears. Perhaps she was here and I just couldn't see her.

It was a beautiful morning that Sunday when I began lessons. The first dog up was learning to gather on a long outrun. Nell's son, Barack was my ever-reliable assistant. My student stood at one end of the field readying to send her dog, while Barack held sheep for her at the other end.

After a number of gathers the student dog was tired and needed a break. My next appointment had arrived and they worked up top in the small training pen. So leaving the first student's set of sheep in a course pen down in the field where we'd just worked, I headed up the hill to do my next lesson. Barack stayed behind, lying beside the captive penned sheep, working them in his mind as he so loved to do.

As I worked with the next dog and handler in the small hilltop pen, Xelie's song began to play over and over in my mind. And fifteen minutes or so later, the song still ringing in my ears, we stopped, this dog needed a rest as well.

I stepped out of the pen and started back toward the large field below. Barack greeted me, his tongue was huge, he was hot and tired as if he'd been working the whole time I'd been in the pen.

My first student called out as she approached, "You might want to put him (Barack) in some water. He's been running around and around the back field, making huge circles from one end to the other. He did it over and over. Don't know what he was doing."

I smiled. Barack never did that. If there were sheep penned down below, he never left them unless he came up to see if I needed help in the pastures up above.

Xelie's song still played in my head. It was Xelie I thought. Practicing outruns perhaps? She had watched so many dogs from my bedroom window learning to gather in the pattern Barack had just run for the past fifteen minutes. Perhaps she was running from the opposite end to gather the penned sheep on the other?

Or perhaps she was just running in a young, fast, pain free body just for the absolute joy of it... In any event, it seemed clear that Xelie had just hijacked her second body in twenty-four hours.

And again, like Nell's nod in the Honda the morning before, she had displayed her behavior to someone other than myself, so there would be no doubt as to what had just happened.

And Xelie had sent her song, the song that played in my head, so that I'd know she was here. It was incredible to think that it might actually be true.

Xelie's song continued to play in my head off and on for some time that day, I don't remember for sure how long exactly. What I do remember is the next thought. It was doubt. Maybe I'm hearing the song because I miss Xelie, because it makes me think of her. Maybe it had nothing to do with whether or not Xelie was "here".

And from the moment that thought etched itself in my mind, something even stranger happened. I absolutely COULD NOT REMEMBER the melody for the life of me. It was as if Xelie's song had been entirely erased from my mind.

For the next week, I kept listening for the song on the satellite as I'd come and go from the house. I even sat a few times in the living room just to listen. A number of songs played that had played during Xelie's final days, but not THE song, not Xelie's song. It had played repeatedly prior to her passing, why not now?

For seven days the song never played. Not until the following Sunday. And when I heard it, I knew that was the song. For the remainder of the day, I forced myself to remember. Strange, I know. But the following morning, it was altogether gone once again.

It was another thought, or series of thoughts, that brought it back. The first was, that doubt, doubt was what had erased the song in the first place. I had doubted that the song was Xelie's greeting, it was Xelie's new afterlife, and it would play when she wanted me to know she was near.

I had been arrogant. Maybe too strong a word... But I had thought myself to be in control of the song and the memory of it. Perhaps Xelie and the universe were reminding me about the limits of my control.

They were reminding me to trust, not doubt, what the universe had to offer. Symbolically the message was to listen, otherwise there'd be silence.

And now, now that I understand what Xelie and the universe were saying through this beautiful, whimsical melody; now I can remember the song whenever I want to sing it, or listen to it in my head.

52.

The viewing

I had been in daily contact with Sue. I knew what the past two days without Xelie had been like, and Sue had now been without her son for five days. His body was to be cremated and his memorial service had been scheduled for Wednesday, a week to the day following his death.

But today, Monday July 7th, was the day of the viewing. Sue had fought hard for this opportunity and now the day was here. She could go see her son, and his body that remained, for the very last time. It would be a terribly emotional visit for Sue, but a necessary one. She needed to say farewell; she needed closure.

Sue and I had discussed just a little about some of the things that had happened upon Xelie's passing. Her son came to visit her in the mornings, she had explained. Her gratitude for his presence was contradicted by the pain and grief she experienced over his loss.

On this morning, I would meet Sue at the funeral home, to offer support if she should need. I had written some thoughts in a card, but I also wanted to give her a gift. Not flowers, they'd simply fade and be dead within a week. A plant maybe, something she could gaze over for some time to come, something lasting that would remind her of her son.

As I drove to the funeral home, I was thinking over the options, but none of them seemed right. I didn't know her son, and I didn't know what would remind her of him.

And then the thought occurred to me. In Xelie's last days, I had spent so much time in the "place in between", in between our physical plane and the spiritual realm, trying to help Xelie pass.

It felt as if the door was still open. So as I drove, I asked Sue's son to help me with the selection, and to help me know which plant he chose.

I pulled into the nursery parking lot. Walking through the gate, I realized just how difficult this was going to be. It was a wonderful nursery filled with aisle upon aisle of lush healthy plants.

I waited to see if I could "hear" which direction I should go. Silence. I waited another second or two, then decided to turn right and start with the first aisle. The selection was vast; I wanted something that flowered.

I slowed down for a close look at a shrub, a beautiful cluster of light purple flowers dangled from a limb. It was something lavender. I liked lavender. I waited. Nothing.

So I kept walking. It wasn't long when I came upon a vine, I loved the leaves and something about it drew me. But there were no flowers. Still... I bent down to look at the potholder to see what it was called. "Morning Calm" was typed on the label.

Morning Calm... Perfect name and I was drawn to it. But there

210

were no flowers. I couldn't be sure.

So I kept walking, reminding Sue's son that I needed help so as to select something meaningful to his mother, my dear friend, Sue. I walked for another five or ten minutes and then came across a beautiful red flower. It was on the outskirts of the nursery and it didn't belong with the plant standing in front of me. It was attached to a vine that had worked its way through umpteen plants and now presented this single flower just for me.

It was beautiful. I took a closer look; the leaves were similar to "Morning Calm". I wasn't sure so I went off in search of a salesperson. I found one immediately and led her back to the flower.

"Oh, that's a trumpet vine", she said. "I've got just one left" and off she went, leading the way. She stopped beside a huge, misshaped vine and pulled it out into the aisle. It was too big to fit in the Honda and it didn't look all that healthy.

Hmmm… I led her to Morning Calm and asked her what this was? Her face lit up. "I didn't know we had these", she exclaimed, before telling me it was the exact same plant as the original vine I had showed her with the flower. And printed on the label, just below "Morning Calm" were the words "Trumpet Vine".

This was it. I selected the healthiest plant, knowing this was the plant that Sue's son had chosen. And as I drove out of the nursery parking lot, Morning Calm filling my back seat, I thanked him for his help. And wished that I had known him in this life, a son who cared this much to come back for his mother.

The viewing was an extremely emotional event for Sue. Only she and her Pastor entered the room where her son's body lay. I closed my eyes to meditate, to offer any energy I had that might have been of assist.

All around me people were chattering, about their own experiences with death, among other things. I was surprised at the focus I was able to maintain.

I don't know if my meditation helped Sue that day, although that certainly was my intent. I don't know what the viewing might have been if

I hadn't been present. In any event, it wasn't about me; it was about a mother and her son, saying goodbye, for the very last time, to their relationship in this material world.

After about an hour, Sue emerged from the room. Clearly the experience of the viewing had been necessary and helpful.

We all made our way out into the parking lot where I gave Sue her card and then presented her with the vine her son had chosen. And after I explained all that had occurred at the nursery, she asked, "What color will the flowers be?"

I answered, red. "Red is my favorite color", she smiled. And Red was also the name of her very dear friend whose home she was restoring, the sheep herding icon who had also passed away only nine days before.

If it had not been for Xelie and all that she taught me from the time we first met until the time she passed and beyond, if it hadn't been for Xelie, the gift I had selected would have had no real meaning. And my presence there on that day with Sue would have been very much different. I might have even found myself too busy to have even come.

53.

Xelie's homecoming

It was on Monday July 7th, after returning home from Sue's viewing, that I sat down for the first time in ten years and began to write. Which made Xelie very happy. Because almost every day after that, even still today, she has sent me a sign of encouragement.

It was still dark on the morning of Wednesday the 9th. I wanted to put fresh water out for the dogs, so I moved toward the large bowl in the grass outside my back door. Lying there right beside it was Xelie's first feather. It was stunning, a magnificent adult hawk feather over seven inches long, in perfect condition.

Now what's so odd about a feather you might ask? When I lived in

California and things had become difficult, it was in this period, that I began to find hawk feathers, many, many of them. Almost every walk I'd find at least one.

Back then, I fancied that they were a gift to sustain me. You see according to Indian lore, Hawks are power birds. I took it then as the universe offering support at a difficult time.

Xelie in the shadow of a bird… first picture taken the morning diagnosis was confirmed.

But I had never, in the nine years I have lived in my home here in Texas, never in the nine years Xelie roamed here, never had I found a hawk feather. In fact, there were very few hawks, in contrast to my home in California, where hawks thrived and were a constant sight overhead.

And here on this morning, was a perfect hawk feather, identical to the ones I used to find in California, lying on the grass beside the dog bowl only feet from my back door. I picked it up, a gift from Xelie I was sure.

And from that point forward to the present as I type, I have found feather after feather; almost every day that I have written. For the first four weeks, it was two, two feathers a day. Many, many hawk feathers, and also owl feathers, both baby and adult, and in the past week a variety of other species in addition to those.

A theme of feathers persists. Feathers, to take flight… To soar. "Free as a bird"… Baby feathers – from the very beginning… Adult feathers – to the end… Hawk feathers – power available… Owl feathers – until death…

Okay, enough of the crazy feather theme, you're probably thinking. But it is odd, all these feathers, all of the sudden, when I had never found any prior to that Wednesday.

And then Thursday, another storm, off in the distance, that didn't quite hit, that came from the east, rather than the west which was without doubt more common. I stopped in my tracks at the sight.

There were two distinct, full rainbows stretching the exact width of my property. Two distinct half circles, displaying a spectrum of light, stretching from the ground to the sky, from one end of my property to the other.

I've never seen anything like it – ever…

It was Friday afternoon when the local vet clinic called. Xelie was back, and ready to be picked up. It was an emotional thing, picking up Xelie's remains. They were packaged in a large green bag. I placed the bag on the front seat of the Honda and began the drive home, tears streaming down my cheeks.

It wasn't until I got back in my house that I examined the contents of that bag. Xelie's ashes were contained in a beautiful wheaten colored box, almost Xelie's exact color, decorated with subtle artistic paw prints. And centered on the lid, was her name, carved beautifully into the wood.

I set Xelie's last resting place on my piano just behind her collar that I had placed there on the morning of her passing. It was my monument to Xelie, the most amazing spirit creature I have ever had the privilege to know.

It wasn't until later that I looked at the other material in the bag. The company that had done such a magnificent job with Xelie, her cremation and the rest, the company's name was Rainbow Bridge.

Not necessarily a surprising name for a pet crematory. Everyone's heard of the Rainbow Bridge, the place where beloved pets who have passed away, live free and happy until the day, the day their person passes. Until that day, they wait on the other side of the rainbow bridge...

Xelie, with or without the help of the universe and the powers that be, had created not just one rainbow, but two. She'd created them on the evening before her remains would be returned to me.

Two rainbows. I was waiting for her. And she was waiting for me.

photo by Bob Degus

54.

From here forward

Today, on the last day of the first draft of Xelie's book, I say thank you. Thank you to Xelie for returning to me the pleasure and satisfaction of writing, something I had always loved, not for the outcome, but for the process, for the moment by moment of it.

Thank you for returning to me the value of living in the present, because the past is dead, after all, and cannot be changed. And the future remains to be seen... We can set foot down a path and navigate the terrain, but in the end we aren't in control of the weather, or the landslides or other challenges in between.

In the end, we will arrive at our final destination, knowing that as we traversed our path, we either behaved with love and integrity and caring and honesty – or we didn't. In the end, we will arrive at our final destination either awakened or still sleeping. That's our choice. That's where we have control.

photo by Bob Degus

Xelie was an alpha to all alphas. She taught me more about leadership than any other creature, human or otherwise. She took her job seriously, knowing to be charged with leadership was a responsibility not to be taken lightly.

She was just and fair to a tee, ruling with love and vigilance. She lead with an impeccable balance of kindness and firmness. A balance backed up by her strength and her deep sense of wisdom.

She was never arrogant or controlling for controlling sake alone. In fact she was generous, generous with her toys, with her love, with her care and protection. Her decisions and actions were always made for the good of the pack, plain and simple, never for self-edification or in greed for power.

It was Xelie's example throughout her life, and the extraordinary efforts she made the last four weeks in her body, that first reawakened my sleeping soul.

It was her tenacity, focus and power in the five weeks and three days following her passing, that reawakened me to the awesome mystery that is our universe, both spiritual and physical.

It was her intelligence, creativity, and sense of artistry and humor displayed in her quest to provide evidence of a spirit world beyond, that's left me with no question that the arrogance of humans, and their supposed superiority, is a laughable lie. Creatures of all shapes and forms have intelligence it's only the measure that defines such.

So sitting here in this quiet place, with a quiet mind, I say one final thank you to Xelie. Thank you for giving me a new beginning, a new life.

This is Xelie's gift.

photos by Bob Degus

photos by Bob Degus

ABOUT THE AUTHOR

For over twenty years, Michele McGuire built a career in the film industry. Rising through the ranks to producer, she was nominated for an Academy Award, in the short film category, for Jobeth Williams directorial debut, *On Hope*. She also garnered two Cable Ace nominations for her work on a Showtime series entitled *Directed By...* in which she produced Kathleen Turner and Treat Williams' directorial debuts.

In addition to producing, Michele was also a writer. Amongst her many screenplays, she co-wrote *Another Round* which played for a stint on Showtime. She also wrote and produced an Independent Film entitled *9/Tenths* for which she was awarded "Best Screenplay" by the Baltimore Women's Film Festival. *9/Tenths* garnered a number of other awards, and was singled out for its cultural significance with the honor of being included as part of the permanent collection of the Library of Congress.

In 2005, Michele's love for animals, working dogs in particular, segued into a new career training stock dogs and their handlers. Nationally known, McGuire has worked with and trained thousands of people and dogs in the nine years that followed to the present. Under her tutelage, numerous stock dog and handler teams have made the leap from sheer novice beginners to advanced competitors in the venues of USBCHA, AKC, AHBA and ASCA. She has also rehabilitated a number of dogs with both behavior and working problems.

Xelie's Gift was inspired by one of McGuire's very own dogs, a Picardy Shepherd named Xelie. It was her experience with this very special dog that transformed not only Michele's life, but her approach to training and working with dogs and the people that love them.

Made in the USA
Lexington, KY
08 December 2014